If you are one of that rare breed of humanity who believes everything that is printed in newspapers, this book is not for you.

Reporters, linotype operators, proofreaders are, after all, people. And people, regardless of how hard they try for perfection, do make mistakes.

The entire newspaper industry spent the last half century contributing to this humorous collection of boners. And we guarantee that it will provide you with many a warm and wonderful laugh.

From the foreword by Earle Tempel

PRESS BONERS
is an original Pocket Book edition.

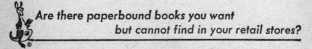

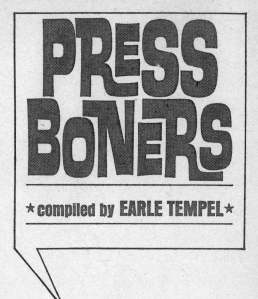

PRESS BONERS

★ compiled by **EARLE TEMPEL** ★

An extensive collection of humorous typographical errors, selected from thousands of newspapers and other media

PUBLISHED BY **POCKET BOOKS** NEW YORK

PRESS BONERS

A *Pocket Book* edition
1st printing.........January, 1967
2nd printing...........May, 1967

This original *Pocket Book* edition is printed from
brand-new plates made from newly set, clear, easy-to-read type.
Pocket Book editions are published by Pocket Books, a division of
Simon & Schuster, Inc., 630 Fifth Avenue, New York, N.Y. 10020.
Trademarks registered in the United States and other countries.

L

This book is respectfully dedicated
to all the people in this world who
say they do not make mistakes.

The typographical error is a slippery thing
    and sly,
You can hunt till you are dizzy, but it some-
    how will get by.
Till the forms are off the presses it is
    strange how still it keeps;
It shrinks down into a corner and it never
    stirs or peeps,
That typographical error, too small for hu-
    man eyes,
Till the ink is on the paper, when it grows
    to mountain size.
The boss he stares with horror, then he grabs
    his hair and groans;
The copy reader drops his head upon his
    hands and moans—
The remainder of the issue may be clean as
    clean can be,
But that typographical error is the only thing
    you see.

Knoxville (Iowa) Express

FOREWORD

THE origin of movable-type printing is clouded in obscurity. Some historians claim that Lourens Coster of Holland invented the first movable-type printing press in 1420. The Germans, however, claim that it was invented by Johann Gamfleisch, of the Gutenberg family, in 1438. Whichever date is correct, it heralded a brand-new form of humor, the typographical error.

Typographical errors, now commonly known as "typos," are caused, to a large degree, by the very human failings of linotype operators and proofreaders as they go about the routine job of getting their paper off the press and on the newsstands. Most typos are unimportant and of little consequence, but occasionally one appears that has a humorous twist. This is uncontrived humor at its best, and many classic typos have been published in the past. Possibly the first typo of any importance happened back in the reign of Charles I of England, when, in a routine printing of the Bible, the Seventh Commandment was printed: THOU SHALT COMMIT ADULTERY. The omission of the little word "NOT" made this edition of the Bible famous as "The Wicked Bible."

Another classic typo of the past is generally credited

to the famous author Bret Harte, who, at the time, was editing a small newspaper in the West. In reporting the death of one of the town's most respectable ladies, he closed the obituary with: "Above all the ladies of this town, she was distinguished for her charity." This came back from the pressroom as "distinguished for her chastity." Harte, being in a hurry, did not make the correction, but put a large question mark on the margin of the proof. The typesetter must have been equally in a hurry, for the final, printed version of the obituary concluded with: "Mrs. McGilligan, above all the ladies of this town, was distinguished for her chastity (?)."

Punctuation can also make a typo. Back in the days when women were fighting for equal rights, a militant suffragette was to speak on the subject: "Woman: Without Her, Man Would Be a Savage." It appeared in the newspaper as: "Woman, Without Her Man, Would Be a Savage."

We also have the classic of all classics, which appeared many years ago in the Boston *Transcript*. The editor was checking the first edition of his paper when he caught the word "navel" in an article about the Boston Symphony Orchestra. Enraged, he stopped the press and ordered the offending word chiseled out of the stereotype. When the *Transcript* appeared on the streets that evening, proper Bostonians were highly surprised to read: "During the performance of this number the kettledrummer sat, like Buddha, regarding his ————."

Will Rogers often said: "All I know I read in the newspapers." That may well have been so. But if you are one of that rare breed of humanity that believes everything that is printed in the newspapers, this book is not for you. Reporters, linotype operators, proofreaders, and other printing-trades employees are, after all, human. And human beings, regardless of how hard they try for perfection, do make mistakes.

Once in a blue moon, a book comes along that is a natural. I like to think that this one may belong in that group. I'd also like to say I wrote this book, but it would not be true. Thousands of the nicest people in the world are its authors. The entire newspaper industry has spent the last half-century writing this book. To them, for many a warm and wonderful laugh, our thanks!

EARLE TEMPEL

PRESS
BONERS

Lettuce won't turn brown if you put your head in a plastic bag before placing it in the refrigerator.

Wildwood-by-the-Sea (N.J.) *Leader*

Mrs. Hawkins, proud of her canning ability, took Reverend Williams to the basement and showed him her well-filled panties.

Mansfield (Ohio) *Tribune*

At the tea party, Mrs. Jones and Mrs. Brown poured at both ends.

Lincoln (Nebr.) *Ledger*

Carlton Pegrim and his son, John, spent most of last week butchering hogs for their neighbors. In four days they kissed more than forty hogs.

Van Buren (Ark.) *Press Argus*

New pews were installed in the church last month. The contractor is now in the process of adding an extension to the parson.

Biloxi (Miss.) *Gulfport Herald*

Williams missed the short infield fly and ended up flat on his grass just back of second base.

Philadelphia (Pa.) *Record*

Just before the court sentence Cockrell was asked if he had anything to say. In a calm voice and without the least sign of emotion he said nothing.

St. Louis (Mo.) *Globe-Democrat*

As a member of this committee, he had made known the fact that nothing should be left undone that might cause any inconvenience to any delegate or visitor.

New York (N.Y.) *Daily News*

It was a perfect day for voting and voters took advantage of it as 4,737 of them went to the pools.

Valdosta (Ga.) *Times*

Mrs. Williams is such a lucky woman; she has been left a widow twice and both times there has been a mourning sale at the stores.

Nashville (Tenn.) *Banner*

Fifty-two others were reported as injured, either by ambulance surgeons who attended them at the

scene of the accident, or by physicians to whom they
went for treatment later in the day.

New York (N.Y.) *Times*

Mike McGrew, deputy U. S. Marshal here, has carried his son's first baby as a good luck charm for 13
years. He has had it hanging on the rear-view mirror
of four automobiles, and during the war, kept it in
the pocket of his army uniform.

Clifton-Passaic (N.J.) *Herald-News*

Shrove Tuesday will be marked by a public supper
featuring pancakes. There will be men flipping the
flapjacks and costumed waitresses.

Baltimore (Md.) *Sun*

When the baby is done drinking, it should be un-
screwed and laid in a cool place under a tap. If
the baby does not thrive on fresh milk, it should be
boiled.

Vancouver (Canada) *Providence*

Mr. John Roberts went to Kansas City last week
with a carload of hogs. Several of his neighbors went
in together to fill up the car.

Kansas City (Mo.) *Star*

Completing plans for the Sunrise services to be held
on Capital Hill, final arrangements were made yesterday. Those attending the hill-top worship service
will be able to return to their homes for breakfast and
have time to dress before Sunday-school.

Walsenburg (Colo.) *Huerfano World*

DiMaggio catches the ball just as his head hit the wall, it drops to the ground, he picks it up and throws to third.

New York (N.Y.) *Telegraph*

An assistant attorney general in Mississippi said he had never heared of anybody being prosecuted under the law.

Augusta (Ga.) *Herald*

Governor Keyser at 35 is the longest Governor in the United States.

(Boston, Mass.) *Christian Science Monitor*

Continuation of government air to farmers, but no specific recommendation for farm-relief bill.

Cleveland (Ohio) *Plain Dealer*

Yesterday afternoon, he read his copy of the *Eagle*. Three hours later he died.

Brooklyn (N.Y.) *Eagle*

Engineers surveying for a railroad in Northern Turkestan have uncovered the skeleton of a massive saurian that must have passed away 3,000,000 years ago last Friday.

Los Angeles (Calif.) *Times*

This car was driven by Sam Kauptman of McKeesport early today when a railroad train struck it at the Eighth Ave., crossing in McKeesport. Mr. Kauptman escaped with minor injuries and shook.

Pittsburgh (Pa.) *Press*

A popular recipe calls for a half-cup of money, two eggs, and a half-cup of chopped almonds.

Dallas (Tex.) *News*

State Law 278 makes it unlawful for hog owners to run at large after July 1st, 1965.

Fort Smith (Ark.) *Southwest American*

The American League standings show the Cleveland Indians in first place with the New York Yankees close up there behind.

Cleveland (Ohio) *Plain Dealer*

A jury recently met to inquire into a case of suicide. After sitting throughout the evidence the twelve men retired, and after deliberating returned with the following verdict: "The jury are all of one mind—temporarily insane."

San Francisco (Calif.) *Chronicle*

Eight candidates, including all four incompetents, are seeking the four City Council positions this year.

Cheney (Wash.) *Free Press*

Of this total, 204 were determined to be from natural causes and 221 occurred in the city of Los Angeles.

Los Angeles (Calif.) *Examiner*

One of Colorado's oldest citizens and a resident of Walsenburg for almost a century died here yesterday. Mrs. Cleofes Quintana was "around" 104 years old at the time of her death, her grandmother said.

Brockton (Mass.) *Enterprise-Times*

The driver of the machine said he swerved his automobile to avoid missing the woman's husband.

Elgin (Ill.) *Courier-News*

Nine youngsters were playing with a stray dog in a field near Rolling Prairie last May when the dog dug up $587 in currency. The children turned the money over to the sheriff but no one claimed it so the sheriff divided it among the nine children. He added a little of his own and they got $60 apiece.

Newark (N.J.) *Star-Ledger*

A big "free feed" at the Democratic State convention, St. Joe, this afternoon. At the "barbecue dinner" will be twenty beef carcasses, 4,000 gallons of hot coffee, 1,000 loaves of bread, 2,000 sandwiches, every variety, and 20,000 fresh bums.

Kansas City (Mo.) *Times*

William Knudson killed four porkers which netted him 1,435 pounds. His mother was with them.

Boonsboro (Md.) *News*

All worshipers are requested to permit ushers to eat them. While to some this may not seem necessary in the interest of good taste and uniformity we request compliance with the practice.

Troy (N.Y.) *Church Bulletin*

The baseball game continued in the cow pasture and ended rather abruptly when a runner slid into what he thought was third base.

Owensburg (Ken.) *News*

Irvin Wilkes was fined $200 and given $30 in jail by Judge Mears after his conviction on a charge of selling liquor.

Portland (Ore.) *Journal*

Into this little town, suffering for months under the effect of the depression, the Judd case has dropped like mama upon the Arizona desert.

Chicago (Ill.) *Tribune*

He [Tampa's new mayor] is an insurance agent and broke.

Pensacola (Fla.) *News*

There are still a few places within the city limits where people are not connected to the sewer.

Grand Forks (N.D.) *Herald*

His death came as a shock for the reason that he was at work as usual on the day he died, and just passed away in his sleep.

(New York, N.Y.) *New Republic*

PRESS BONERS

A Youngstown woman received minor injuries Wednesday night when the car in which she was riding overturned on icy pavement one mile north of Edinburg on Route 14.

Akron (Ohio) Beacon Journal

Both men were examined by veterinaries, and immediately shot by Humane Society officers.

Newport (Vt.) Express

CORRECTION

Unfortunately, the illustrations of edible and poisonous types of mushrooms were reversed on Page 14 of our Sunday edition.

Chicago (Ill.) Tribune

It was on a bleak and wintry December 21, 1620, that our Pilgrim ancestors first set foot on Plymouth Rock. In their honor it has been the custom for more than a century and a half to celebrate December 21st as Forefather's Day. The first commemoration of this day was held at the Old Colony Club in Plymouth in 1769. The food which was placed on the table that afternoon would undoubtedly have provided a whole winter's fare for those early Pilgrims. Their menu was as follows:

Large Baked Indian

Pittsburgh (Pa.) Post-Gazette

The women on the local team were doing fine until the last half of the fifth when all the bags got loaded.

Muskogee (Okla.) Times-Democrat

Several witnesses for Judge Frech testified that Mrs. Brougham's reputation wasn't what one would call spotless. She was accused by one dignified housewife of having milked a cow clad in pink step-ins.

New York (N.Y.) *Evening Journal*

Judge Boyd told Ginn to "Take the affidavit and go to hell." So Ginn and Fuller went to Austin to the Court of Criminal Appeals.

Houston (Tex.) *Press*

Mr. Kermott never married. He was a member of the Church of Christ, but in later years, due to his illness, did not take an active part in church affairs. Surviving are two sons, three grandchildren and one great-grandchild.

Nashville (Tenn.) *Tennessean*

Rev. Brown announced that after the program they would have a pot-luck supper. All women giving milk are asked to come early.

Montgomery (Ala.) *Church Bulletin*

While the car is a wreck, its occupants can be truly grateful that they escaped with their lives. The tree is badly scared.

Warwick (N.Y.) *Advertiser*

The son of the deceased Assessor is to succeed his father as successor.

New Orleans (La.) *Times-Picayune*

After her first date, she was no longer a virginian.

Los Angeles (Calif.) *Times*

Of all the peanut growing states, North Carolina has the largest yield per ache.

New Britain (Conn.) *Herald*

A 72-year-old man, furious because his $65 shoes pinched his feet, fired six pistol shots into the Los Angeles store where he bought them, but the bullets went wild.

No one was injured in the fusillade of shots fired yesterday by Bernard Schwartz who was seized by a newsboy when he tried to flee from the store, his pistol empty.

Detective Eugene Dansforth said Schwartz told police:

There's a quick and delicious way of preparing eggplant. Wash and dry the vegetable but do not peel; then slice about ¼ inch thick. Dip slices in flour and cook in a skillet in hot butter.

Alexandria (Va.) *Gazette*

George Grant is the proud possessor of a brand new Chevrolet sedan and also a new wife, having traded in the old one for which he received a liberal allowance.

Logan (Ohio) *Republican*

Three hundred deafmutes sang "The Star Spangled Banner" with their hands. They had no trouble reaching the high notes.

Toledo (Ohio) *Blade*

Through the check rigging the Federals come through with 30 percent of the cost of $7.68 per day per patient, a bunch of imbeciles.

Albuquerque (N.M.) *Tribune*

Mousam Lake is well filled with guests this month.

Sanford (Me.) *Tribune*

Walter Whitworth, who recently sold his business interests in Hartford, together with his family, returned this week to his farm near Cromwell.

Hartford (Ky.) *Ohio County News*

Upon arriving at the Honolulu airport, the two men were presented with coveted lays by several Hawaiian maidens.

Chicago (Ill.) *News*

Miller's ice-house caught fire, and though a determined effort was made to save the building from flames, it burned to the ground. With it 20,000 pounds of ice were reduced to ashes.

Peterboro (N.H.) *Transcript*

Miss Lavalle will become the bride of David Brown of White Plains Saturday at St. Mathias Church, Bedford Hills, at the Parkview Hotel, Mt. Kisco, at 4 p.m. A reception will be held or when you are angry or emotionally upset. Don't drive when you drink

Chappaqua (N.Y.) *New Castle Tribune*

PRESS BONERS

Officials of the Catonsville Community College have decided to stop necking on the campus on weekend evenings. In other words, all that kissing that has been going on under their noses has to stop.

Baltimore (Md.) *Sun*

His first venture into the antique field was in Asheville, N.C. There he met his wife.

Denver (Colo.) *Rocky Mountain News*

Folks have written in asking how to control males in gardens.

Hutchinson (Kan.) *News-Herald*

One felt how fortunate Burlington is that concerts of this caliber are so rare.

Burlington (Canada) *Gazette*

She said that anyone who doesn't have a ride, can get one to or from the station for a feel.

Laramie (Wyo.) *Post-Register*

Now we are abandoning our University freshman test to use the College Broads altogether.

Austin (Tex.) *University of Texas Daily Texan*

And listening to this music one can almost see those gallant, hardy Puritans on the little deck of the Mayflower as she steamed into the harbor.

Easton (Pa.) *Express*

26

An Indian woman squatted over a fire in one tepee, and you could smell fresh meat cooking.

Wichita (Kan.) *Eagle*

Our football boys last season had a good line, plenty of weight, and plenty of speed in the backfield. The trouble was they had no lass defense.

Latham (Kan.) *Leader*

Served with a writ yesterday afternoon, B. O. Blake must produce children in court within twenty-four hours.

Wildwood (N.J.) *Leader*

When washing walls or woodwork, fasten a washcloth around your waist with a rubber band. The cloth will keep water from running down your arm.

Portsmouth (Me.) *Herald*

She wore tortise-rim glasses with gold and silver trim on them, a large wedding band set with five goodsized diamonds and false teeth.

Little Rock (Ark.) *Democrat*

Kim Novak's romantic life has made rather dull copy since her idyll was nipped in the but.

Las Vegas (Nev.) *Optic*

The wedding of Miss G. S. and K. K. took last Saturday.

Le Sueur (Minn.) *News-Herald*

Mrs. Fischer's dog follows her car to the restaurant where she works and sleeps under the automobile all day.

Minneapolis (Minn.) *Star*

Miss Neta Halloran, noted trick rider and rodeo performer, will exhibit her elaborate silver-mounted prize waddle at the J. B. Marion Store all day Saturday.

Creighton (Calif.) *Daily Mirror*

To remove coffee stains place stained part over a bowel and pour boiling water into it from a height.

Chattanooga (Tenn.) *News*

Miss Dee David also was wounded in the fusillade.

New York (N.Y.) *Herald-Tribune*

The dog came bounding down the lane, emitting whelps at every bound.

Wildwood (N.J.) *Leader*

The Duchess of Winsor counteracted rumors by kissing her husband (the Duke) eight times on the gangplank.

St. Petersburg (Fla.) *Times*

It always has seemed to me that death must be the most exiting of all adventures.

Buffalo (N.Y.) *Courier-Express*

Milk now sold in public eating places must be in the original containers.

South Bend (Ind.) *News-Times*

Each girl wore a big orange letter on her seater and together they spelled E-L-K-I-N-S.

Williamson (W.Va.) *Daily News*

Church school at 9:45. We begin a new year with new literature on Sunday. This is a good time to start that child that you have promised yourself for so long.

Alpena (Mich.) *News*

9:00 WNBW—Television Playhouse: 'Somethings Got to Give,' based on Marion Hargrove's navel.

Washington (D.C.) *Sunday Star*

Toilets are available in the gymnasium only. If you are interested in arrangements for reservations contact the office of the Dean of Students for written approval.

Temple (Tex.) *University News*

Harry McAllister, a patient at St. Joseph's Hospital, Highland, became ill a few days ago.

Belleville (Ill.) *Advocate*

The solons just passed an ordinance which stated, "It shall be unlawful for any person to park any vehicle in a metered zone without having first deposited the proper coin therein."

Pueblo (Colo.) *Chieftain*

29

The all-important tourist traffic has deceased over 40 percent.

St. Petersburg (Fla.) *Times*

Miss Dorothy Morrison, who was injured by a fall from a horse last week, is in Saint Joseph's Hospital and is covered sufficiently to have her friends come to see her.

Morristown (N.D.) *News*

All the goods saved from the ruins was a bushel of potatoes. They escaped only in their night clothing.

Sayre (Pa.) *Times*

Miss Ansley James Newman of Pasadena, Calif., will be interested to learn of her engagement to Mr. Robert G. Thomas, Jr.

Seattle (Wash.) *Times*

Both high school bands will be present to dispense with fine music.

Barnesboro (Pa.) *Star*

Gearty said he and Sjolberg talked with Norton about five minutes trying to persuade him to put the gnu down, but he kept the officers covered.

Lebanon (Pa.) *News*

Despite the fact that an open safety-pin is working its way through her sister, little Nell Clark of Austin-

ville, near here, today was apparently little the worse
for her experience.

Vicksburg (Miss.) *Post*

A sixty-five-year-old male with proven eosinophilic
gastroenteritis was followed for nearly seven years.

(Chicago, Ill.) *Journal of the AMA*

Mrs. Thurston Gaylord and daughters are planning
to tour the Black Hills, Yellowstone Park and other
places of interest. They are taking a tent and cooking
utensils and will vamp by the side of the road.

Vivian (S.D.) *Farmer*

The fire company was called to the home of Car-
roll Sparks, basketball coach, Wednesday afternoon.
Considerable damage resulted.

Logansport (Ind.) *Press*

Mr. and Mrs. Walter F. Hill announce the coming
marriage of their daughter Helene. No mate has been
selected for the wedding.

Wilkes-Barre (Pa.) *Leader News*

Obviously a man of sound judgment and intelligence,
Mr. Rau is not married.

New Bethlehem (Pa.) *Leader-Vindicator*

A typical scene of Colombian rural people taking
their produce to open air markets. The man carrying the sack probably contains potatoes.

Nashville (Tenn.) *Banner*

The Reynoldsburg Band will assist as usual in the Memorial Day program and will add snap to the occasion. Nothing adds dignity to a Memorial band.

Reynoldsburg (Ohio) *Record*

The Centerway lot will follow the pattern of other lots as far as parking fees are concerned. The meters will permit parking at ten dents per hour.

Corning (N.Y.) *Leader*

He said the baby was a light green sedan which bore New Jersey license plates, and was sitting between the two men.

Richmond (Ind.) *Palladium-Item*

Hardly had this episode occured when Shaukart's son appeared with a knife and made his alleged threat to cut off the priest's head if the latter performed the ceremony. This would have been the greatest insult possible to any Mohammedan.

New York (N.Y.) *World-Telegram*

Suicide by poison, 50; poison gas, 29; hanging, 185; drowning, 30; firearms, 124; cutting or piercing instruments, 18; jumping from high prices, 7.

Chicago (Ill.) *Tribune*

Adolph Peerson is suffering from an injury of his left eye. Mrs. Peerson's sister of Ellendale is a guest in their home.

Wahpeton (N.D.) *Farmer-Globe*

Mr. and Mrs. Jerome Smith and children left Sunday for Wichita, where they will take treatments for his ears, and the family will enjoy the show.

Follett (Tex.) *Times*

Mr. John Trimble, of the George Washington University, said he had found England a wonderful country, especially the cathedrals. When he stood in Westminster Abbey he had really thought he was in Heaven until he turned around and saw his wife standing by his side.

New York (N.Y.) *Times*

The garbage and two nearby storage sheds were saved from the fire.

Idaho Falls (Idaho) *Post-Register*

The young bride-elect is a has been residing at 250 Fifth East Street.

Salt Lake City (Utah) *Deseret News*

And they were married and lived happily even after.

Fort Smith (Ark.) *News*

She held out her hand and the young man took it and departed.

Boston (Mass.) *Transcript*

A Census Bureau report revealed that southern girls do marry at an early urge.

Memphis (Tenn.) *Commercial Appeal*

Sweet potatoes are in abundance. Some Irish potatoes of excellent quality from Maine are on the market. Bankers from Idaho are plentiful and a little down in price this week.

Chattanooga (Tenn.) *Times*

Pumping of steam from a threshing machine engineer has been continuous for several days and probably will be continued.

Council Bluff (Iowa) *Nonpareil*

The bride-elect and her mother were in the deceiving line.

Clovis (N.M.) *News-Journal*

When the Beatles appeared on the hotel balcony, the crowd swept through police lines and steel barricades in a crumbling wave Uh
a crushing wave.

Sydney (Australia) *Herald*

Japanese welcomed their new constitution by happily mobbing Emperor Hirohito while their band played the famed U. S. military march *Stars and Strikes Forever.*

Wallace (Idaho) *Press-Times*

Miss Harrison, a senior at Alabama College, is a member of Phi Alpha Mu, an honorary music sorority. She will graduate in June with a major in piano and a minor voice.

Montgomery (Ala.) *Journal*

The New York State Conservationist has published a list of pointers on what to do if you should become lost in the woods. The fifth and last recommendation: "Don't yell, don't run, don't worry and, above all, don't quit. Better yet—write to the Forest Service, U. S. Department of Agriculture, Washington, D.C., and ask for their pamphlet No. O-23, 'What to Do When Lost in the Woods.' "

New York (N.Y.) *Daily Mirror*

O. E. Plummer won a 30-pound turkey at the shurkey toot Saturday.

Tulsa (Okla.) *Tribune*

Captain Devereux is a real hero. He stood on the bride until the crew had left.

Worcester (Mass.) *Gazette*

Mrs. Homer Cotton discovered a berry bush bearing both purple and red raspberries. And Mrs. Stanley Palmer—to mention another freak of nature—has an apple tree with apples and also blossoms and buds.

Victor (N.Y.) *Herald*

Electrically operated registers which accept only nickles, dimes, and tokens and drivers clad in new fitting uniforms, are other outstanding features.

Jackson (Miss.) *Clarion-Ledger*

Bradbury K. Thurlow of Winslow, Cohn & Stetson, Inc., says that unless the market gains enough vigor for a new surge forward it can be expected to either do nothing or decline.

Washington (D.C.) *Post*

Insull heard himself assailed as a self-centered financial executive who buttered his own beard.

Terre Haute (Ind.) *Tribune*

Warren Olliff and Mrs. T. Johnson have recently joined Bunte Brothers, as sales representatives, according to F. A. Bunte, president. Mr. Olliff will cover northern Texas and Oklahoma and Mrs. Johnson.

(New York, N.Y.) *Candy Industry*

At the launching of the Queen Mary, one of England's proudest luxury liners, a British Broadcasting announcer made this observation: "From where I am standing, I can see the Queen's bottom sticking out just over her water line."

Quebec (Canada) *Chronicle Telegraph*

Breaking the glass with a chair he climbed through and clung to the sill by his fingerprints until three detectives called on him to jump.

New York (N.Y.) *Times*

Several chorus girls told the police they thought the prizefighter was simply pinch-drunk.

Pittsburgh (Pa.) *Press*

Friends of Harry Schmidt will be sorry to learn that he had been for the past week at his home in Main Street.

Monongahela (Pa.) *Republican*

Prime Minister Dudley Senanayake resigned today. His retirement was attributed to acute stomach trouble aggravated by political opposition.

Los Angeles (Calif.) *Times*

Rev. and Mrs. G. C. Bidwell and children of (find out where) are visiting Mrs. Bidwell's father, J. L. Boggs.

Little Rock (Ark.) *Democrat*

The chief is inclined to believe that a crossed wife might be the cause of the fire.

Scranton (Pa.) *Times*

Mr. duPont spoke graciously of his prospective son-in-law, Franklin Roosevelt, Jr. "He seems like a pretty nice buy," he said.

Pittsburgh (Pa.) *Post-Gazette*

Three years late, they were married in 1938.

Seabrook (Tex.) *Suburban Journal*

After returning from their African safari, the two men showed their guests the many interesting photos of the large breasts they had found in the jungle.

Houston (Tex.) *Chronicle*

37

Crows raise havoc among game birds . . . One of the easiest and most satisfying types of off-season shooting is blasting crowds with a shotgun.

Portsmouth (Va.) *Star*

Dwarf fruit trees are also a small garden solution, since one of them will usually fit the space that three normal trees require.

Bakersville (Calif.) *Californian*

"We were jammed from the time the sale started until the doors closed at midnight," announced a Walgreen executive. "People were driving round the parking lot waiting for empty spaces. While they waited they ran across most of their neighbors!"

Deerfield (Ill.) *Star*

The report of the commission is illuminating and also very depressing. It says that "wages are admittedly high in the United States, but so is the cost of loving."

Lake Charles (La.) *American Press*

Latest market reports reveal that mines are down, airplanes are slightly up and tobaccos closed strong.

New York (N.Y.) *Daily Mirror*

In business correspondence you may assume that any signature not preceded by (Miss) or (Mrs.) is a "Ma."

Santa Barbara (Calif.) *News-Press*

After taking on water and a brief walk about the city the boat is scheduled to depart.

Deland (Fla.) *Sun-News*

He then attempted to shoot himself in the head but the bullet apparently only creased his scalp and ran out of the tavern and drove off.

Fairmont (W.Va.) *Times*

The Federal Government has been called into the Chicago crime situation to afford police a new weapon for ridding the city of its bald men.

Albany (N.Y.) *Evening News*

Mrs. Clara Wiggins was suddenly taken seriously Wednesday morning at the home of her mother.

Eugene (Ore.) *Register-Guard*

A heart specialist examined the President and a specialist on international disorders was called in.

Beaver (Pa.) *Beaver County Times*

Housepests for several days at the Lindau home are Mr. and Mrs. Wally Burman of Sioux Falls, South Dakota.

Fosston (Minn.) *Thirteen Towns*

Fire of unknown origin completely destroyed the home and contents of Mr. and Mrs. Howard Smith.

Corona (Calif.) *Independent*

Following a wedding trip to New Orleans the couple are sorted and marked by volunteers throughout the year and stored until Fair time.

St. Louis (Mo.) *Globe-Democrat*

Miss Elaine Rhodes entertained at her home with a household shower honoring Miss Elaine Rhodes.

Hendersonville (N.C.) *Times-News*

Several deer hunters in the north woods area in the past week have been shot at by mistake for wild animals lighting cigars.

Lincoln (Nebr.) *State Journal*

He is president of the Southwestern Irritated Cotton Growers.

Las Cruces (N.M.) *Sun-News*

"I believe, too, that individualism and the profit system will prevail, which means an opportunity for every man and woman to live his or her own life, working toward financial independence by industry and theft."

Albany (N.Y.) *Knickerbocker News*

A British firm has built the world's smallest radio tube. It does not work.

Detroit (Mich.) *News*

The Highams, now residents of Fillmore, came here May 6 to open an applesauce repair shop on Santa Clara St.

Fillmore (Calif.) *Herald*

Jack Ader has joined the sales staff of Pat Hartly. His precious associations were with Patricia Fair and Ann Barry.

(New York, N.Y.) *Women's Wear*

The Pan-American Bank, of California, with commercial asses of $2,200,000 and savings of $2,217,123, closed its door today.

Frederick (Md.) *News*

On the new keyboard, the vowels, for example, are all placed on the second row, where typists' fingers normally rest.

Washington (D.C.) *Times-Herald*

The Erie Barge Canal, traversing upstate New York, is used primarily to carry wheat and oil from the Great Lakes to New York and oil and wheat from New York to the Great Lakes.

Walden (N.Y.) *Citizen Herald*

Representatives from about 14 of the town's package stores met last night to hear some advice about how they can protect themselves from Police Chief Herman O. Schendel.

Hartford (Conn.) *Times*

County Policeman Grizzle requests us to state that all persons caught running a car under 16 years of age, or a person running a car drunk will be prosecuted.

Atlanta (Ga.) *Journal*

Mrs. Brown is visiting her sister, Mrs. Smith of East Queen Street, who is ill with an absence in her head.

Chambersburg (Pa.) *Public Opinion*

Mrs. Annie Besant, eighty-year-old theosophist, was confined to bed today at the home of friends at Wimbledon. A severe child forced her to cancel all lecture engagements.

Houston (Tex.) *Chronicle*

He left for a vacation at his lodge, taking his favorite two great dames with him.

Pico (Calif.) *Gazette*

An incipient forest fire drew workmen, today, from the task of mastering a burning gusher which had killed nine men and destroyed oil statisticians estimated in value up to $200,000.

Hibbing (Minn.) *Tribune*

The bride-elect was showered with pieces of her chosen china.

Sequin (Tex.) *Gazette*

When hunting deer in the freezing cold of the Colorado mountains, be sure to take along a waterproof matchbox full of watches.

Denver (Colo.) *Rocky Mountain News*

Alcohol, taken in sufficient quantities, produces all the affects of intoxication.

Brookline (Mass.) *Chronicle-Citizen*

Another 1.35 million acres, now desert, could be irrigated and made arable. In addition, 700 thousand acres now irrigated by ancient methods and yielding but one crop a year could be brought to yield two crops in three years.

Washington (D.C.) *Post & Times Herald*

With this new paste, women with copper bottoms will no longer have any trouble keeping them shining like new.

Calgary (Canada) *Herald*

Brief radio advices from the steamship Montauk which rescued the men in Unimak Pass, reported that oiler Poiey of Seattle had gone crazy from the five-day battle with an Alaskan stork.

Boston (Mass.) *Evening Globe*

The whiskey was poured in the gutter and the men placed in Lebanon jail. Over 150 gallons have been poured out of Mr. Boyd in the past week, all going through to West Virginia points.

Roanoke (Va.) *Times*

He then shot himself in the stomach and jar.

Clermont (Fla.) *Press*

Deer hunters are plentiful, and several have been shot in this vicinity.

Bradford (Vt.) *United Opinion*

In the course of his work Mr. Smithson went to the balcony office and unlocked the safe preparatory to placing it in the cash box for the day.

Livingston (Mont.) *Enterprise*

Mrs. Boike returns to Germany for visit with family after 57 years. At Frankfurt they were met by relatives and used for silage feed for livestock.

Cedar Falls (Iowa) *Record*

Up among the clouds nestling in the heart of the Davis mountains, it is an ideal vacation spot winter or summer. The altitude is 6,000 feet either summer or winter.

Bryan (Tex.) *Eagle*

In the course of the visit, he talked with Mrs. Horton. He left the place without saying anything to her.

Alma (Ark.) *Times-Herald*

Ninety percent of big city dwellers lie and act exactly like their small town cousins.

Augusta (Ga.) *Chronicle*

Chicago has had the largest conflagration in its history since the famous cow of Betsy Ross kicked over the lamp in the gay 90's.

Chicago (Ill.) *Tribune*

Shooting should be excellent in traditionally favorite spots.
Kill Kill Kill

(New York, N.Y.) UPI Dispatch

This raised the question of adherence to civil air regulations limiting the flight time of pilots and crows to eight hours a day.

New York (N.Y.) *Wall Street Journal*

Here's the recipe for "French Egg Nog": two egg yolks, two tablespoons of sugar and two jiggers of cognac in a tall warm lass.

Portsmouth (N.H.) *Herald*

Luther Burbank did so much toward improving the health value of many of our common fools.

Chicago (Ill.) *Defender*

Have you ever tried this recipe for keeping your furniture looking new? Add one tablespoon turpentine and three tablespoons of linseed oil to one quart of boiling water. Let cool and apply any other polish.

Denver (Colo.) *Rocky Mountain News*

Rotarians from all over southern Vermont and New Hampshire started their two-day annual district conference Friday, and heard Jack Pride of Bristol, England, a director of Rotary International, say "Wisdom is the greatest thing, but in its getting, also get understanding. Rotarians must be prepared to think, and drink, and think."

Rutland (Vt.) *Herald*

Chief Baker was on a ladder feeding a horse through a second-floor window when flames flared up, burning him on the face.

Saratoga Springs (N.Y.) *Saratogian*

45

On Station KABL, Oakland Calif: "After this announcement, we will continue with our uninterrupted music."

San Francisco (Calif.) *Chronicle*

It was rather pleasant to hear their voices and realize that they were 3000 miles away.

Meredith (N.H.) *News*

Five distinguished guests were present in the persons of Dr. James S. Spur and Dr. L. S. Mudge.

Danvers (Ill.) *News*

The New Year was ushered in by Pomonans with sounding of whistles and automobile horns, and with general nosemaking at dances.

Pomona (Calif.) *Progress Bulletin*

The new device automatically couples air and steam hose between passengers and freight cars.

Los Angeles (Calif.) *Times*

Among the first to enter was Mrs. Clara Adams of Tannersville, Pa., lone woman passenger. Slowly her nose was turned around to face in a southwesterly direction, and away from the hangar doors. Then, like some strange beast, she crawled along the grass.

Burbank (Calif.) *Post*

Mr. Denny tried to sell the commissioners some bridge timbers. After lots of lickering they finally agreed on a price of $45.

Guntersville (Ala.) *Advertiser-Gleam*

The rise of wheat prices resulted in a brisk trade as farmers began to move their long-stored grin.

Bismarck (N.D.) *Tribune*

Blueberries are getting more plentiful and several were seen starting off with pails this morning.

Amesbury (Mass.) *News*

If not convenient to move furniture outdoors to clean, place a damp cloth over the piece of furniture and then beat it.

Atlanta (Ga.) *World*

Chairman Bowman next requested the members to indicate by a show of hands that they had or had not received a copy of the Council's 'By-Laws.' Very few members had or had not received a copy of the Council 'By-Laws.'

Baltimore (Md.) *News American*

We wish to thank our many friends and neighbors for their kind assistance in the recent destruction of our home by fire.

Laramie (Wyo.) *Boomerang*

6:00 KBIQ—"Music for Nervous 'pPeoj', elomcs: Nervous People.

Los Angeles (Calif.) *Times*

The two minutes' silence at eleven o'clock on the morning of Armistice Day, November 11, is to be broadcast throughout the United Kingdom by the British Broadcasting Company.

Pittsburgh (Pa.) *Press*

Pauline Taunton is entertaining the same evening in a similar manner, for her younger sister, Evelyn, one of the autumn debts.

Philadelphia (Pa.) *Bulletin*

He said he couldn't see how DC Transit could operate if the subway system "skims the cream off the milk and takes the gravy."

Washington (D.C.) *Post*

At work today at his new job as general manager of the Gilpin Air Lines, Elliott Roosevelt, son of President Roosevelt, said he would devote 78 hours a day to his work until he found out what was expected of him.

Saginaw (Mich.) *Daily News*

George Hampton left last week for a business trip to Memphis. He probably will be away until full.

Nashville (Tenn.) *Tennessean*

In the interior of Sumatra, rice is sown by women who let their hair hang loose down the back in order that the rice may grow luxuriantly and have long talks.

Pomona (Calif.) *Progress Bulletin*

After an hour rinse thoroughly in warm water in which a large lump of soda has been dissolved, afterward boiling thoroughly in cold water.

Omaha (Nebr.) *World-Herald*

After locking your door (leave the key as far as it will turn after locking) then put the wife over the doorknob and through the little hole in that old skeleton key! The key cannot possible be turned from the outside then!

Aberdeen (S.D.) *American-News*

At Wednesday's luncheon meeting of the Guilford Rotary Club, to be held at Chello's Restaurant on the Post Road, Jacob Emery will speak about his experiences in the Arctic. Because of snow and cold weather last Wednesday, Emery was unable to be at the meeting.

New Haven (Conn.) *Register*

The fire broke out while the parents were milk cows in the barn.

Columbia (S.C.) *State*

Helen Traubel will be so-lost with the NBC Symphony this afternoon at 5:30 on KRIS.

Corpus Christi (Tex.) *Caller*

The blond stripper was grinding to a halt under the blue spot when we walked in and grabbed a table. There was really no need to grab it, for it was Monday night and there were only three other people in the big room, half of them waiters.

Pasadena (Calif.) *Independent*

Keep away weeds. It is best to weed on a hot, dry day when the plants are dry. Never work in the garden when the pants are wet as that is the best time to spread disease.

Narragansett (R.I.) *Times*

Much can be done at home. Use the following methods:

Stoves—Scour inside and outside with crude oil and steel wool. Scrub gas openings with soap and water, and clean with a stiff wife.

Charleston (W.Va) *Mail*

Rev. Hammond was congratulated on being able to get his parish plastered.

Tujunga (Calif.) *Record-Ledger*

Mr. and Mrs. Charles L. Thompson and Mr. and Mrs. Russell Hartwick of Tampa will entertain at open house Sunday, from three until tight.

Clearwater (Fla.) *Sun*

Lowell Thomas lectured on the Palestine and Arabian campaigns (1919), accompanied the Prince of Wales on his Indian tour (1922) and has spoken over the radio without intermission since 1930.

New York (N.Y.) *Times*

The new president of the Optimist's club is prominent in all civic affairs. and has been one of the greatest roosters for the newly completed Woman's Club.

Alhambra (Calif.) *Times*

Mr. Matthews is in Clay, Texas, where he is taking the place of the Santa Fe Railway for two weeks.

Oakdale (La.) *Journal*

No matter if your coming trip is by ship or plane, it's nice to know what the weather will be like when you get to your destruction.

Denver (Colo.) *Post*

Tully V. Foster, owner of the Club Casablanca, said he paid Miss Rand $1,000 to dance with her fans. These are ostrich, six or seven plumes, 41 inches long, with a potential wingspread of 82 inches. Among her fans one night were a state liquor agent, a reporter, and a radio newsman.

Houston (Tex.) *Post*

Ladies, remember the HDC Christmas party at our house Friday, the 12th, beginning at seven. Pot-luck supper will be served. Bring your husbands and gifts to exchange.

Bruce (Miss.) *Calhoun County Journal*

Baldness may be caused for many reasons: a local attack of disease, shallow soil (a rock present underneath the sod), chinch bugs or the doings of a dog.

Lancaster (Pa.) *Sunday News*

Any woman can be more attractive and charming . . . but . . . and that is that awful big but we are talking about.

Cincinnati (Ohio) *Enquirer*

While mowing the lawn the other day Mrs. Richesin had to work on the lawn mower and somehow got her thumb in the mower and broke it.

Paducah (Tex.) *Post*

An old dirty, shabby tramp, standing on the curb, his dingy coat tied with a huge safety pin, struggling with a beautiful red nose, trying to get it into his threadbare lapel.

Kansas City (Mo.) *Star*

I have had so much trouble this year that I have grown six months older.

St. Louis (Mo.) *Globe-Democrat*

Possibly the worst thing that could happen to a voo-doo believer is for the leader to put a nurse on him.

New Orleans (La.) *States & Item*

Contest rules are that snapshots must be of a person not larger than 8 x 10 inches.

Muskogee (Okla.) *Times-Democrat*

It is only a snake in the grass who will attempt to knife a man in the back with so evil-smelling a report.

New York (N.Y.) *Daily Mirror*

McConnell went out into the Quebec forest wearing only a trunk.

Itasca (Minn.) *Iron News*

There were no inhabitants east of the Pueblo of Pecos until 1794. West of the Rio Grande there were even less.

St. Louis (Mo.) *Globe-Democrat*

Dr. Frank Willard Libby, the newly-appointed scientist member of the Atomic Energy Commission, is known as the inventor of the 'atomic time clock', a device by which he has been able to determine the ages of objects up to 20,000 years old. This device will be used in Egypt as well. . . . There it will be possible to determine the age of the mommies in Egypt.

Chicago (Ill.) *Tribune*

The groundhog always sees his shadow in Nebraska and if the tradition holds good we are doomed to six weeks of mighty disagreeable weather in February.

Norfolk (Nebr.) *News*

Surrounded by all the royal baronesses, duchesses and countesses, Mrs. Dellamont said she felt like a plain ess.

Cleveland (Ohio) *Plain Dealer*

City police were called to rush a woman to Oil City Hospital for delivery of a child after the woman failed to obtain a cub in three calls.

Oil City (Pa.) *Derrick*

Mrs. Glen Golden is general chairman of the affair. Mrs. LeLand Ax and Mrs. Ben Gordon have charge of invitations. Mrs. John Estrich, Mrs. E. J. Ries and Mrs. Harold Stevens have charge of Harold Stevens.

Angola (Ind.) *Steuben Republican*

His face was a striking one, and even without his clothes people would have turned to look at him.

Littleton (Colo.) *Independent*

Only three jockeys—Eddie Arcaro, Ted Atkinson and Jess Higley—have ridden Nashua in his 15 races. He has won for each boy. He's now pitching for the Redlegs.

Winston-Salem (N.C.) *Journal*

Mrs. Eleanor Roosevelt conferred with Mrs. Randolph Guggenheimer and Lansdell K. Christie, co-chairmen of the $100-a-plate dinner for Adlai Stevenson at the Waldorf-Astoria, April 25. Stevenson will make a major campaign address at the affair.

Daily double paid $37.50

New York (N.Y.) *Post*

A well-known beauty expert says that beauty is not a question of age. It's making the best of one's good paints.

Honolulu (Hawaii) *Advertiser*

His left thumb, which was shot away, is doing nicely.

Chattanooga (Tenn.) *News-Free Press*

The Sudan, a 1,000,000-square mile territory about the size of western Europe, lies to the south of Egypt. It is populated by about 9,000,000 people, a third of them jungle tribesmen.

The headwaiters of the Nile are there.

Baltimore (Md.) *Sun*

TODAY'S WEATHER: H$_2$O!

Fort Smith (Ark.) *News*

We've got fifty yankettes married into English nobility right now. Some of them are duchesses. Some are countesses. Eleven are baronesses. Only one is a lady.

Boston (Mass.) *Globe*

A British scientist predicts that, in time to come, men will be born toothless.

New York (N.Y.) *Times*

Two girls who have been friends for many years and do many things together had babies the same day.

St. Paul (Minn.) *Pioneer Press*

Mrs. and Mrs. Edward Smith of Red Hook became the parents of a daughter on Tuesday at Vassar Hospital, Poughkeepsie.

This is the end of Red Hook.

Rhinebeck (N.Y.) *Gazette*

He wore a stickpin in his purplish tie and shiny shoes.

Detroit (Mich.) *Free Press*

55

The winner's were Fun For Two, I'm Expectin' and Sandra's Baby, in that order.

Detroit (Mich.) *News*

Miss Dorothy Killien is claimed by beauty experts to have the smallest waist of any girl in the screen colony. Her waist measurement is only 21 inches in diameter.

Baltimore (Md.) *Sun*

Push back the cuticle with the orange stick dipped in liquid cuticle remover or oil. While you do one hand, soak the other.

Hagerstown (Md.) *Herald*

Mrs. Jones let a can-opener slip last week and cut herself severely in the pantry.

Pittsburgh (Pa.) *Post-Gazette*

In Nyack, all activities ceased at eleven o'clock, and for two minutes all stood in silent contemplation of the day. Three silent short blasts on the fire whistle brought notice that the time had arrived.

Nyack (N.Y.) *Evening Journal*

Fair Board members and friends are to have a 'work night' on Thursday. Those participating are urged to wear clothes and bring tools.

Sandusky (Ohio) *Register*

THE WEATHER: temp. hrd hrdl hrdlu hrdly hrd h hO.

Milwaukee (Wisc.) *Journal*

The solitary moorland inn of Chequers at Slape Stones, in the Hambledon Hills, has just lost its landlord, but the turf fire on its open hearth is still kept burning, as it has been since it was kindled under Queen Anne.

London (England) *Times*

McDonald, given a blood transfusion, is the father of four children.

Raleigh (N.C.) *News and Observer*

The Nov. 26 meeting of the Business and Professional Women's Club will be held at the home of Mrs. Miller. . . . If this happens, it might be wise to put out the old faithful mouse trap and keep them under control.

Nampa (Idaho) *Free Press*

It was not a heartening picture. He walked alone back to his hotel, undressed and showered and went down to dinner.

(Philadelphia, Pa.) *Saturday Evening Post*

Hope, whose wife made one of her bare public appearances while presenting the cup to the winner, was surrounded by no less than eight Kentucky state policemen.

Cincinnati (Ohio) *Enquirer*

She and her husband unended the child and shook him in a vain effort to dislodge the participle.

Youngstown (Ohio) *Vindicator*

America is now witnessing the rise of the great meddle class.

Norfolk (Va.) *Virginian-Pilot*

While working in the flower garden last Thursday, Mrs. Johnson bent over to pick a lucky four-leaf clover as a bumblebee flew up her dress and stung her on the

Van Buren (Ark.) *Press Argus*

The Naval Observatory said the comet, a ball of white-hot gas, speeding 100 miles per second, probably was not visible to the naked.

New York (N.Y.) *American*

The font so generously presented by Mrs. Smith will be set in position at the east end of the Church. Babies may now be baptised at both ends.

Boston (Mass.) *Globe*

She recently broke her leg between the levee and the ankle.

Peabody (Kan.) *Gazette-Herald*

The first event today was the administering of the oats of office to County Judge Milton D. Richardson.

Brownsville (Tex.) *Herald*

Men's Activity Night Starts March 25 in the Girl's Gym.

Mountain View (Calif.) *Pictorial News*

Mrs. MacIvor has urged that all parents attend this meeting and bring the youngsters and other problems.
Coos Bay-North Bend (Ore.) *World*

Hundreds of school children had climbed the mountain with their teachers and rucksacks on their backs.
Bethlehem (Pa.) *Globe-Times*

Valeria is 17 and giving us nothing but hearache.
Lancaster (Pa.) *New Era*

He came to Sherman, Texas, when a boy and had liver at Mineral Wells for fourteen years. He had written twelve books.
New York (N.Y.) *Journal-American*

Our advertisers are reliable and do not necessarily subscribe to the opinions expressed in this publication.
Abingdon (England) *North Berks News*

A think like that makes a fellow feel old.
Minneapolis (Minn.) *Tribune*

The church is now forming a Little Mothers Club. All women desiring to become Little Mothers are asked to meet with the pastor in his study after services.
Monroe (La.) *Church Bulletin*

The newest thing in syndication is the Scripps-Howard leased wife.
Denver (Colo.) *News*

A parent in the United States is good for 17 years.

Albuquerque (N.M.) *Journal*

May Irwin, nationally and internationally known as one of the greatest American comediennes, is celebrating her sixty-sixth birthday at her summer home near Clayton, as has been her custom for several years.

Watertown (N.Y.) *Times*

The 205th Tank Battalion of the 27th Armored Division started its third full day of training today at Camp Drum.

Troops were up for revelry at 5:30 a.m.

Troy (N.Y.) *Times Record*

One official said an alarming number of U. S. Troops were not taking marijuana.

Philadelphia (Pa.) *Inquirer*

Walter P. Reuther said today that the next major bargaining goal of the Automobile Workers Union was a shorter work week with no reduction in say.

New York (N.Y.) *Times*

In America there are at the present time 84 known men who resemble Abraham Lincoln, and make their livings largely by impersonating ham.

Topeka (Kan.) *Capital*

After being hit by the DeWitt car, she tripped on the curbing and fell flat on her

Fort Smith (Ark.) *Times Record*

A critic of our churches says that they are 'dominated by a lot of old hens.' Does he refer to the lay members?

Nashville (Tenn.) *Southern Lumberman*

And for the first time, a potential Negro ballet of 154,000, jumping more than 50% since 1952, gives candidates something new to think about.

Dallas (Tex.) *News*

Miss Nickerson has been attempting college in Wichita.

Salina (Kan.) *Journal*

From the three, Miss Velma Sorrells, Miss Morena Stallard or Miss Mary Ann Parker, two virgins will be selected for the Christmas Pageant.

Tupelo (Miss.) *Journal*

He is not very old, because he started when he was a mere boy.

New York (N.Y.) *Journal-American*

The boys will be grouped at the base of the tree and will be carted away the next day by the coeds to be distributed to the poor children at their party on Saturday night.

Chicago (Ill.) *Crane College Javelin*

Movable type for printing was made from clay in China about 10:40 A.M.

Morristown (N.J.) *Daily Record*

"Do you know what it is to sit down of an evening with a book in your hand, your faithful dog in your mouth, and your good pipe at your feet?"

Brooklyn (N.Y.) *Eagle*

I would like to ask for a little information concerning a birthday party I am to give. There will be six couples. I would like to know if it is proper for the hostess to take the gentlemen's clothing on entering the house or to take them into the bedroom so as to deposit their clothing where they wish.

Newark (N.J.) *News*

Dr. Gilbert Murray, O.M., will celebrate his ninetieth birthday quietly at his home at Boars Hill, near Oxford, tomorrow, with his wife, Lady Mary Murray. They have been married 66 years.

This evening he is to broadcast in the BBC Home Service a talk called "Unfinished Battle."

London (England) *Observer*

We are studying for our Sunday School lesson, "The Ten Virgins." "Each one bring one" is the slogan for Sunday School.

Marion (Ill.) *Republican*

Uniforms with medals will be worn at the reception of General Allan Brewster, Tuesday evening. Trousers optional.

Norfolk (Va.) *News*

On the broad sidewalk in front of the White House a throng of pickets, some of them nuts, marched in a circle.

Washington (D.C.) *Star*

The blond young actress who bares a striking resemblance to her famous mother.

Nashville (Tenn.) *Banner*

The accident was reported as purely accidental.

Vandalia (Mo.) *Leader-Press*

The climax was reached as President Eisenhower and Vice President Nixon appeared on the rostrum and acknowledged a thunderclap of tears.

Camden (N.J.) *Courier-Post*

The men's dormitory will house 160 single men and will include a number of papartments for married students.

Des Moines (Iowa) *Sunday Register*

A mud room is a special de-mudding spot where the kids can shed their muddy shoes, and wash their outdoor garments, kick off their face and hands.

Galesburg (Ill.) *Register-Mail*

The twins are enroute to Afghanistan with their faster parents.

Akron (Ohio) *Beacon Journal*

She returned to her studio, called her friends to a party, and unveiled the new nose. Her guests toasted it.

New York (N.Y.) *Times*

Five nights a week a Daily day editor and froof-reader spend between three and eight hours at the print shop checking for such errors.

San Jose (Calif.) *State College Spartan Daily*

Happy birthday to Galen Graham, who was delight-fully surprised by a few couples last evening who whiskied him off to Wichita Country Club.

Wichita (Kan.) *Evening Eagle*

From a WAC recruit's reference: "She is noted for her ability to work hormoneously with others."

San Francisco (Calif.) *Chronicle*

Safety Hazard—old ladies should be replaced with new ladies in Winfield Foundry. An experimental geared ladle will be purchased.

Detroit (Mich.) *Dodge Main News*

The report of the U. S. Employment Service that nine out of every ten veterans seeking work are now painfully employed is a good one.

Troy (N.Y.) *Observer-Budget*

The episode provides the actor with a beautiful roll and fortunately for the play, he's more than equal to the task.

Albuquerque (N.M.) *Journal*

The taxi crashed head-on into the auto driven by Jack Brillinger. Mr. and Mrs. Brillinger and Mrs. Smith were severely injured, and were removed to the hospital, both cars suffering severely, the engines having interlocked through the force of the smash. They were reported this afternoon to be resting easily.

Boston (Mass.) *Traveler*

Three special trains Thursday carried Mayor "Big Bill" Thompson to New Orleans.

Birmingham (Ala.) *News*

After the recent riot in Foochow, China, the resident Methodist bishop there cabled home. "Wife left for Manila. Everything quiet here."

Kansas City (Mo.) *Star*

W. A. Knapp and Rev. Solomon motored into Pecos Tuesday, to interview a dentist that has been giving Bro. Solomon trouble since his arrival in the valley.

Balmorhea (Tex.) *News*

The bed in which Abraham Lincoln slept in a Rockford, Illinois, hotel during his debate with Stephen A. Douglas has just been sold for $20.

New York (N.Y.) *Times*

City Collector Taylor was to post the names of delinquent taxpayers today. These will be published in the local paper, June 22, and offered for sale July 3, if still delinquent.

Washington (D.C.) *Daily News*

In Wilmington, Del., recently, the local Power Squadron class was taking an oral quiz and the instructor asked a female student, "What signal would you give if you were coming out of your slip slowly stern first?"

The class recessed without delay.

Wilmington (Del.) *Sunday Star*

Bozeman each year watches that age-old spectacle of young men passing through the transition period from carefree youth into developed manhood and womanhood.

Bozeman (Mont.) *Chronicle*

Be sure to undress baby properly in hot water.

Houston (Tex.) *Chronicle*

Today there are 2,300,000 members of the Girl Scouts of the U. S. A. Of these, 1,750,000 are girls.

(New York, N.Y.) *The American Girl*

"The author of Foreever Amber, Kathleen Winsor, has written another book, Star Money, that is called a "Twentieth Century Amber," and is supposed to out smell the two million copies of the first book."

Tulsa (Okla.) *Daily World*

Please bring gifts suitable for chicken from the cradle up to fourteen years of age.

Upper Sandusky (Ohio) *Chief-Union*

Gregory Speaker celebrated his fifth birthday Monday with the aid of 12 fiends.

Coldwater (Mich.) *Daily Reporter*

Major General T. B. Larkin, Army Quartermaster General, ordered a study of possible further reductions in Army rations. The chief of the subsistence section will fake the investigation.

Long Island (N.Y.) *Star*

I am writing this letter to the Culver Citizen to tell the people of Culver the facts about the members of the sympathizing union who were picketing the Culver telephone exchange last Thursday night . . .

As long as those seven men are in the Culver exchange our Culver girls will walk the street. Think about that, Culver citizens.

Culver (Ind.) *Citizen*

"A Self Portrait" the color film on the life and work of Rembrandt, turned out by him in association with Auerbach Film Enterprises, has reached completion and is now ready for distribution.

New York (N.Y.) *Daily Mirror*

He uses pancake makeup to cover his freckles and other scares.

Los Angeles (Calif.) *Herald-Examiner*

In a report submitted by the Home Mission Board earlier today it was said one of the Church's greatest needs at the present time was to increase millionaries'

salaries. Many of them were finding it difficult to provide for even the bare necessities of their families,
the report said.

Toronto (Canada) *Star*

Linda, 14, suffered a fractured left foot and cuts on
her fact.

Seattle (Wash.) *Times*

This time Truman wet all out for Averell Harriman.

Columbus (Ga.) *Ledger*

Gov. Wilbur Cross said that this was his first visit
to beautiful Lake Waramaug and its wonderful state
park, but he hoped it would be his last.

New Milford (Conn.) *News*

Twice during the day the President walked to the
Executive offices in the band-box sort of structure at
the western end of the White House, once to look
over his maid and again just before going to church.

New York (N.Y.) *Times*

Dr. Stratton constantly tells how disgusting these
things are which he asi m rdleu upeupetupumons.
They are disgusting, and no preacher should discuss
disgusting thing in public in this way.

New York (N.Y.) *Times*

Dr. Samuel I. Bechdel, the scientist who put a
"widow" in a cow's stomach to prove the animal's
ability to produce vitamin B complex, died yesterday.

Reading (Pa.) *Eagle*

She is a junior at the University of Maine where she is working for a bachelor.

Bangor (Me.) *Daily News*

Sheriff's deputies arrested a woman who has been receiving county welfare aid for three of her four children and a former cab driver on abortion charges.

San Francisco (Calif.) *Examiner*

Your reply to W. U. solves my problem. Ten days ago I made a trip, feeding our 18-months-old child kept hot in a vacuum bottle for six hours.

Syracuse (N.Y.) *Post-Standard*

"Spend your Saturday Nights at the Hacienda and your Sunday mornings in bed with a Progressive Alaskan."

Ketchikan (Alaska) *Progressive Alaskan*

Simultaneously with Mr. Bayes, Miss Belle Cramer is showing some landscapes and still lives.

New York (N.Y.) *Daily Mirror*

It is a curious sight when the gardens are in bloom to watch dozens of artists squatting on their easels.

Daytona Beach (Fla.) *News-Journal*

Man was sent into this world to earn his living by the sweat of his brow. You didn't find Adam walking about the Garden of Eden with his hands in his pockets!

Cincinnati (Ohio) *Church Bulletin*

PRESS BONERS

Woman live about three times longer than men in the United States.

Oakland (Calif.) *Tribune*

"I'd like to have my name in the paper." Standing on Second street a 701-year-old veteran of the roads made this declaration.

Woodland (Calif.) *Democrat*

The Presbyterian Women's Club had a birthday party for Mrs. Learnold Craft. When noses were counted, 17 were turned up.

Van Buren (Ark.) *Press Argus*

Two more Mills brothers, Donald and Douglas, 17 year-old twins, join U. S. Army. They join their twin brothers, Edward and Richard and Robert.

Genesee (N.Y.) *Livingston Republican*

The WAC sergeant was telling the new group of recruits how to conduct themselves at the base and ended with this statement: "If you're going to do anything to disgrace your uniform, take it off."

Fort Smith (Ark.) *News*

With the dock strike being over, dock workers are returning to work on docks running from New York to Texas.

Houston (Tex.) *Post*

Before viewing the premiere of the film, the journalists will be quarted at a downtown hotel.

Chicago (Ill.) *Tribune*

Members of his church have presented Rev. Smith with a new 1964 Chevrolet. He asks the prayers of all his congregation.

Russellville (Ark.) *Courier-Democrat*

Twenty-five head of cattle owned by Almer Johnson were accidentally fed sodium chloride which had been mistaken for salt. Two of them died.

Minneapolis (Minn.) *Star*

Owing to the good condition of the roads in this locality, our weekly worship of Almighty God has been discontinued.

Deadwood (S.D.) *Church Bulletin*

After leaving the club he collapsed on the sidewalk and died without medical assistance.

New York (N.Y.) *Times*

High school students had an assembly session Monday morning with Anna Bird Stewart, author. Principal Roscoe Coyne said he hadn't seen a high school audience so taken in by a speaker in years.

Hutchinson (Kan.) *News-Herald*

By order of the selectmen, cows grazing by the roadside or riding bicycles on the sidewalks is hereby forbidden.

Norway (Me.) *Advertiser*

The game began promptly forty-five minutes late.

Cincinnati (Ohio) *Enquirer*

71

Mrs. George Padrnos' name was intentionally omitted from the list of guests attending Mrs. Frey's birthday party last week.

Lake Andes (S.D.) *Wave*

It won't be a real New England clam chowder unless you put your heart into it.

Boston (Mass.) *Traveler*

The union is seeking a ten percent wage increase plus improved benefits and double time for any day in which the workers work.

Philadelphia (Pa.) *Evening Bulletin*

Judge Walter Thompson warned the manufacturers that the courts had already handed down the decision, and he would look with disfavor upon anyone who tampered with his union suit.

New York (N.Y.) *Times*

Eleanor Parker plays opposite him in this birth-provoking adventure in modern marriage.

Dubuque (Iowa) *Telegraph-Herald*

John Falter passed away quietly in his sleep. Survivors are his wife, two daughters and one song.

Fort Smith (Ark.) *Southwest American*

On the criminal side of the ledger, the court clerk reported 1,171 cases filed. Ninety-three criminal asses were tried between Jan. 1 and June 30.

Phoenix (Ariz.) *Gazette*

The engineer of the train put on full steam, dashed up against the cow and cut it into calves.

Auburn (Ind.) *Star*

While the infield has made several improvements in the lineup, the outfield is still the shame that it was.

St. Louis (Mo.) *Post-Dispatch*

The Women's Birthday Club met to help celebrate Mrs. Smith's birthday. As the club had been organized for a year and all of its members had had birthdays this year and there would be too few in the next few years, it was decided to discontinue the club.

Kansas City (Mo.) *Star*

Sunday breakfast meeting has been planned for the official board of the church, with the Rev. Mr. Blank undressing the group.

Jackson (Miss.) *State Times*

For animal shapes, use covered ice-cream molds, or chill in deep pants and cut out with animal cookie cutter.

Miami (Fla.) *Daily News*

About one out of seven workers in the U. S. is rated as skinned labor.

Greensburg (Pa.) *Tribune-Review*

I work for the Pittsburgh Natural Gas Company. Over ninety percent of the people in Pittsburgh have gas.

Pittsburgh (Pa.) *Press*

This was only his second appearance on a Nantucket stage, but he has already established a reputation which he will not find difficult to maintain.

Nantucket (Mass.) *Inquirer & Mirror*

The murder of the young girl in the basement of our church last Saturday night has caused some criticism among members of our congregation.

Atlanta (Ga.) *Church Bulletin*

Max Sorensen is survived by six sisters, two brothers and partly cloudy skies promised for the morning.

Wichita (Kan.) *Eagle*

Mrs. Clinton was one of those fine young people endowed with a personality that eradicates sunshine and happiness whereever it goes.

New Hampton (Iowa) *Economist*

Female students who marry during their course will not be permitted to remain in college. Further, students who are already married must either live with their husbands or make other arrangements with the dean.

Cleveland (Ohio) *Plain Dealer*

OFTEN MISPRONOUNCED: Architect. Pronounce ar-ki-tekt, a asi, h a n aoietashrdet aoshrAO as in ah, i as in it, accent first syllable, and not arch-i-tekt.

Charlotte (N.C.) *Observer*

In baring women undergraduates, Case is reverting to its original prewar policy.

Poughkeepsie (N.Y.) *New Yorker*

Warden Tippit who was slain during the break when the fugitives engaged in a running gun fight, came into court with his entire right arm and shoulder in a plaster cast.

Omaha (Nebr.) *World-Herald*

The seventh meeting of the Knox County Jersey Boosters was held at the home of Katherine and Maxine Cochran. The group inspected the girls' calves.

Mount Vernon (Ohio) *News*

While Gerry was running down the first-base line, the umpire kept a closed eye on the action.

Jackson (Mich.) *Citizen Patriot*

Mrs. Freddie Preston entertained a group of children Saturday in honor of her little daughter's third birthday. About 20 children were present.

Mrs. Freddie Preston entered the Wellsboro Hospital late Sunday afternoon for observation.

Corning (N.Y.) *Leader*

Dundee crossed the room, stepping over the dead man's neck—a swank affair of dark, polished wood, with a heavy knob of carved onyx.

Alton (Ill.) *Evening Telegraph*

Police today were notified that the police in Alma had found the purple woman's bathing suit in a locker at the country club.

Van Buren (Ark.) *Press-Argus*

Mrs. Dora Meyer, believed to be the oldest woman in New Jersey, and among the oldest in the country, died at the age of 116. The aged woman had outlived three husbands and attributed her long life to the fact that she ate a dozen each day.

Newark (N.J.) *Star-Ledger*

Fifteen men were charged with a new Black Legion kidnaping today in a warrant asked by the Prosecuting Attorney, who said that three of the men had been taken into custody. He said one of the three had confessed that Wilkins, of Ecorse, was abducted, tied to a tree and lashed.

The final 36-hole round will be played tomorrow.

New Britain (Conn.) *Herald*

The drive for entrants will be continued throughout the next two months with a dairying mass-meeting to be held within two weeks at which time a purebred bull heifer will be given away.

Oxford (Miss.) *Eagle*

There have been many ballplayers who have been able to handle the bat from either the left or right side of the batter's box. However, most sportswriters agree that Mickey Mantle is the greatest swish hitter of all times.

New York (N.Y.) *Daily News*

Charles Kirkpatrick is able to resume his studies after a siege of romantic fever.

Walla Walla (Wash.) *Union-Bulletin*

Mrs. Fred Watson of Fayette Street is all at her home.

Quincy (Mass.) *Patriot-Ledger*

Miss Snyder told her audience that in her tour of the devastated countries she found the people suffering intense hardships and that many were dying of salvation.

Rockway (Pa.) *News Bee*

The clerk was struck while taking a nap with what police believe was a blackjack.

Palm Beach (Fla.) *Post*

We wish to thank neighbors and friends, and especially the members of the K.K.K., who so kindly assisted in the death and burial of our father and uncle.

New Castle (Pa.) *News*

The report came back that the courthouse, jail and public officers were in a very dilapidated condition.

Somerset (Pa.) *Daily American*

There were a number of women in the audience that looked on as they were run through the auction ring.

Texarkana (Tex.) *Gazette*

Ray W. Fleming, druggist of Tonopah and Reno, encountered a range cow traveling by auto with his wife.

Tonopah (Nev.) *Bonanza & Goldfield News*

The Japanese team wants $2,500 plus broad and room.

Gastonia (N.C.) *Gazette*

Mrs. Fred Moulton has a poultice on her head and the doctor told her to soak it every hour.

Fort Smith (Ark.) *Times Record*

Mrs. White is assisting in the care of her mother in Iowa, so Mr. White is straying at the local hotel.

Plymouth (Ill.) *Tri-County Scribe*

Few families listed as worthy of community support have less than 100 cans of fruit and vegetables stored in their panties.

Grand Island (Nebr.) *Daily Independent*

Miss Grace Shipley is being wired for electricity, which will be a great improvement and add considerably to her value in the community.

Fort Smith (Ark.) *News*

Situated on the banks of Lincoln creek, the mill draws its power from a large dame.

Omaha (Nebr.) *World-Herald*

Among the gifts of the bride to the bridegroom was a beautiful dressing down.

Boston (Mass.) *Transcript*

An auto truck loaded with cheese was stolen during the night from the garage of the Fellsway Cheese Company at 40 Garfield Avenue, Somerville. The police are on the scent.

Boston (Mass.) *Transcript*

The Federal Personnel Manual carries this revealing sentence; "The death of an employee automatically ends his employment."

Washington (D.C.) *Post*

The members of the church showered Reverend and Mrs. Hooten last Saturday night.

Clovis (N.M.) *Church Bulletin*

Pat and Erica Steel, madam of the highpriced call girl ring, have been the objects of a nationwide search since the Court of Appeals voided Jelke's conviction and ordered a new trial because press and public were barred from the first one.

Miss Steel also was giving detectives a chaise.

New York (N.Y.) *Post*

We have our own farm at Landover, Md., and on it a very fine herd of cows, from which much of the milk, pumpkins, fruit and other ingredients of our products are obtained.

Washington (D.C.) *Star*

Aspromonte gave a stimulating exhibition afield and at bath in the absence of Charlie Neal, nursing a pulled groin.

Los Angeles (Calif.) *Herald-Express*

Mrs. John Post is pretty sick at her ranch west of town and all persons are requested by her sons to stop coming to see the big hog until she improves.

Anaheim (Calif.) *Bulletin*

Preparations of savory, tempting meals for the soldiers will consume about 1,000,000 pounds of spices this year. That's the report of Mary I. Barber, fool consultant in the office of the Quartermaster General in Washington.

Washington (D.C.) *Post*

To separate two glasses which have stuck together, fill the inner one with cold water and the outside one with warm water.

Philadelphia (Pa.) *Inquirer*

The modern telephone truck which you see so often is a vertical machine-shop. The devices it carries include a boring machine for digging holes, a derrick for raising them, etc.

Cleveland (Ohio) *Plain Dealer*

The calls started at noon Saturday night.

Columbus (Ohio) *Dispatch*

I keep on burning in my kitchen all night and it takes very few kilowatts.

Augusta (Ga.) *Chronicle*

The International Telephone and Telegraph Co. announced the development of a complicated device which can tell men from women.

Klamath Falls (Ore.) *Herald & News*

Then the officers closed in. Murphy was wounded in one hip. A stray bullet killed one bystander slightly.

Maryville (Mo.) *Forum*

Following her arraignment before the United States Commissioner, Mrs. Fields, 30 years old, of Miami, Florida, admitted to reporters that she had intended bootlegging in New Jersey the 306 bottles of whiskey which were found in her at Matawan.

New York (N.Y.) *Times*

The minister said that the church widows were a disgrace to the parish and it was time somebody washed them.

San Francisco (Calif.) *Examiner*

He returned to his duties Monday after several weeks' absence due to his death.

Altoona (Pa.) *Tribune*

WEATHER FORECAST: Colder tonight, heavy frost if clear. Saturday fair, probably followed by Sunday.

Mount Carmel (Pa.) *Item*

Mrs. and Mrs. James Evoy have returned from a week's fighting trip in Wisconsin.

Springfield (Ill.) *State Register*

The foursome took in a number of shows and enjoyed the gal life of the city.

Bethesda (Md.) *Journal*

The managers of the two Brunswick toy factories will put on night shirts next week.

Rutland (Vt.) *Herald*

Never forget the power of understatement; it is the greatest unused force in advertising.

(New York, N.Y.) *Printer's Ink*

Harry Longley, resident here off and on for a number of years, writes he has left town to accept a job elsewhere, but will return in the fall at which time he will repudiate his just debts, dollar for dollar.

Anchorage (Alaska) *Times*

PRESS BONERS

Officers of the Transcontinental Oil Company, the Mexican subsidiary of the Standard Oil Company of New Jersey, have been reopened.

Philadelphia (Pa.) Public Ledger

And the stock exchange stresses that the volume of short interest represents less than one tenth of one percent of the hares listed on the exchange.

Idaho Falls (Idaho) Post-Register

Coney, usually the strictest, this year permits gentlemen to bathe without trunks.

Dallas (Tex.) News

RACE RESULT:

Oh Rosie	6.80	3.20	2.80
Will Ya		7.40	3.40
Squeezit			2.60

Mobile (Ala.) Register

After 24-48 hours' filtration, the pool becomes so clear that when the water is calm you can read 'heads' or 'tails' on a dame lying 8½ feet below the surface.

(New York, N.Y.) Swimming Pool Annual

Nearby was the food table, presided over by Mrs. Herbert Cunningham, all in white, and filled with luscious cakes and cookies.

Boston (Mass.) Herald

Mrs. David Tyler, Miss Janice Porter, Miss Elizabeth O'Meara, and Miss Nancy Corden sail today from hamburg gravy, buttered wax beans, bread and butter, frosted graham crackers.

Springfield (Mass.) *Union*

A special "Old-Fashioned Night" is scheduled for Friday, when men who attend will be asked not to wear suits or neckties.

La Salle (Ill.) *Daily News-Tribune*

Eleven of the 20 children were boys. Fourteen are living and seven married.

San Francisco (Calif.) *Bulletin*

The husband opened the telegram and read: "Twins arrived tonight, more by mail."

Little Rock (Ark.) *Democrat*

Chris Rumpel suffered several broken and bruised legs last night when a sled on which he was riding struck a tree.

Troy (N.Y.) *Record*

The life guard, although off duty at the time, saw the man's plight and plunged in after him, although he was dressed for the street. He rescued this man, and today he has a wife and baby.

Macon (Ga.) *Telegraph*

Dr. Briggs is once more among us for a brief season. He says and does exactly as he thinks right, without

regard to the opinion and belief of others. His wife
is not with him.

Burlington (N.C.) *Times-News*

A number of Eves, members of the LaSalle county
home bureau, who startled the community around
Streator last year by establishing in a sylvan retreat
where the hand of man was not allowed to set foot.

Chicago (Ill.) *Daily News*

A. J. Tobin of Clymer Auto Co., spent 30 days
last week at the Ford plant.

Hudson (Wisc.) *Star Observer*

The luncheon was an elaborate one, and at its
close automobiles took the visitors on a yachting trip
around the bay.

San Francisco (Calif.) *Examiner*

Mrs. and Mrs. Seligman have lied most of their
married life in Hartford.

Hartford (Conn.) *Times*

The courses were established for high school
graduates who are out of work as a result of meetings
of the New London Chamber of Commerce and the
State Labor Dept. Both refresher and beginner courses
will be offered.

New London (Conn.) *Day*

He is a retried executive of General Motors.

Long Island (N.Y.) *Star-Journal*

A number of Mrs. Durham's lady friends surprised her at her home on Fourth Avenue last Friday evening with a miscellaneous shower. The guests were entertained with a mock wedding, after which Mr. and Mrs. Durham opened the guests.

Three Forks (Mont.) *Herald*

Extended weather forecast for today through Wednesday, March 16:

Eastern Pennsylvania, Eastern New York and Middle Atlantic States: Temperatures will average 6 to 10 degrees above normal in the southern portion and 3 to 6 above normal in the northern portion, colder tonight, and Elysburg R. D. 1; Mrs. Eva Lahr, warmer Sunday and colder Monday, Tuesday and Wednesday.

Sunbury (Pa). *Item*

Miss Swanson is in the hospital this morning after having being bit yesterday by a spider in a bathing suit.

Mansfield (Ohio) *Tribune*

Two experiments in this line are noted by the papers, one conducted by a man in Brooklyn, his machine having four wings like a bird.

Indianapolis (Ind.) *News*

There's a nudist camp in Cajon Pass, Calif., where girls are required to wear something while swimming. It's covered in the camp regulation, "Swimming: All girls, and ladies regardless of age, must wear bathing caps in the pool."

(New York, N.Y.) Associated Press

Jockey Eldon Nelson was aboard Smart, which finished first by two lengths. Gun Bow was second with Tenacle third. Nelson paid $10.80, $2.40 and $2.20 Gun Bow paid $2.20 and $2.20 while Tenacle returned $2.20.

Fort Smith (Ark.) *Times Record*

SAUCE FOR BROILED MEATS

One-half pound butter
Juice of one lemon
One-half bottle A-1 Sauce
One-fourth to one-third cup STRONG black coffee

Melt the butter in the sauce-pan or small skillet; and stir ask your physician for advice on further treatment.

Cincinnati (Ohio) *Post*

Mrs. Bertha Bradley entertained the Ladies' Social Club. She asked the ladies to come dressed like tramps and that was easy for most of them.

Sparta (Ill.) *News-Plaindealer*

Miss Heine wore a bluey-green jumper, with a bandeau to match, and Mrs. Peacock wore a determined expression on her face.

London (England) *Morning Post*

Mr. and Mrs. Smith have a daughter, Judith Maxwell, born on November 5th in Charleston, W. Va. After finishing in the West Virginia project, they moved back to New England in February.

Bangor (Me.) *News*

A 36-year-old New York school teacher became the bride of a 77-year-old New York minister and the father of nine children in this city late today.

Syracuse (N.Y.) *Post-Standard*

It is remarked that the number of deaths of celebrated men this year has been exceptionally low. This suggests to us also that not a single birth of any famous person has been recorded the past twelve months.

New York (N.Y.) *Times*

The bombing occurred at 11:40 p.m. while a party was in progress in the place. A minute before the explosion, several of the party had opened the window and placed their heads outside to cool off. Their heads were still outside when the blast occurred.

Kenosha (Wisc.) *Evening News*

He was found unconscious by a neighbor who smelled gas and two maintenance men.

St. Petersburg (Fla.) *Times*

Mrs. and Mrs. Shipman spent Saturday in Kansas City shoplifting for Christmas.

St. Joseph (Mo.) *News-Press*

The father is a Moron. That's one reason the family wants to live in Utah.

Terre Haute (Ind.) *Tribune*

The Mid West is suffering from one of the worst cold-spells in years, with temperatures dropping as low as twenty degrees below zero. Tomorrow's forecast is for continued mild.

Oklahoma City (Okla.) *Times*

The Misses Doris, Agnes and Vivian Smith are spending several days at the home of their mother. This is the first time in years the community has had the pleasure of seeing the Smith girls in the altogether at one time.

Sidney (Ohio) *Daily News*

There was something about that title, Old Incestors' Trading Corporation, that inspired confidence.

New York (N.Y.) *Journal American*

A dishonest promotor takes no financial risk in mailing unordered merchandise to prospective donors. The promotor usually negotiates a deal with the supplier of the merchandise. He gets (Sylvia Porter is on vacation) a good-sized commission from the supplier and also retains ownership of the merchandise if it is returned.

Kalamazoo (Mich.) *Gazette*

Prior to his return to work this morning he spent the weekend at his fiancee's home and is now back on the job better versed in business methods.

Waterbury (Conn.) *Republican*

Miss Sylvia Clifford is returning home by train as she gets seasick every time she flies.

St. Louis (Mo.) *Post-Dispatch*

Miss Winifred Leeming, 321 West Olive Street, was the honoree at a linen shower given Wednesday at her home as a prenuptial courtesy. Her marriage to William Schultz, W. B. Phillips, and Robert Smyers, of Genola, Kansas, will take place in the near future.

San Diego (Calif.) *Union*

Capt. W. R. Hinchcliffe and Hon. Elsie Mackay, third daughter of the wealthy ship builder, Lord Inchcape, hopped off from London Tuesday in an attempt to fly to New York. The flyers have not arrived in New York and it is believed they fell into the Pacific Ocean.

Sherman (Tex.) *Democrat*

Children who can not swim unless accompanied by father or mother are not allowed at any time.

Chatham (N.J.) *Courier*

When numerous small articles are to be washed, put them in a discarded nylon stocking, making a knot at one end, and then place the articles in a washing machine. This way, it's easier to fold in two egg whites beaten still and sweetened with one-fourth cup of sugar. Garnish lightly with unsweetened chocolate, grated. This serves six.

Holyoke (Mass.) *Transcript-Telegram*

Nor do many Chicago women wear their jewels any longer. Instead they lock them up in safety vaults and go about with cheap imitations or nothing at all.

New York (N.Y.) *World*

She wore a shapeless house dress and stockings rolled down to the angles.

Los Angeles (Calif.) *Times*

A surprise pink and blue shower was given Mrs. L. Ross Tuesday evening. After Mrs. Ross opened the gifts, the big surprise came. She told those present that she was not expecting.

Lancaster (Ohio) *News-Review*

The members of the clinic stated that more than a hundred babies had registered with many complaints.

Philadelphia (Pa.) *Bulletin*

Several hundred feet of wife were attached to the device and it is believed this was the mechanism used to wreck his home.

Jacksonville (Fla.) *Times-Union*

Kermit Marston, thirty, former resident of Covina, is believed somewhere in California tonight unaware he has been bitten by a rapid dog.

San Francisco (Calif.) *Examiner*

Persons living on Rogers Avenue, Brooklyn, were awakened at 2 a.m. today by the explosion of gas fumes in a manhole in front of 55 Rogers Avenue. The manhole was hurled through the plate glass window of Ralph's barber shop.

New York (N.Y.) *Sun*

Members of the Junior team are unsettled tonight and Friday; slightly warmer Friday and in northwest portion tonight.

Fayetteville (Ark.) *Northwest Arkansas Times*

This place is known as the preferred resort of those wanting solitude. People searching for solitude are, in fact, flocking here from all corners of the globe.

(Boston, Mass.) *Christian Science Monitor*

North Alabamians are more and more exploring the scenic attractions in their own backyards. Many will tour the cool taverns with which North Alabama is bountifully blessed.

Albertville (Ala.) *Sand Mountain Reporter*

Last year this time, 1,435 men and 690 women were seeking unemployment.

Cape Breton (Canada) *Post*

When agents for both the buyer and the seller perform services for their clients, both agents are entitled to be paid for their efforts. That's what brokers are in stock enchange transactions—agents. The buyer pays his agent a commission and the seller pays his brother a commission.

Albany (N.Y.) *Knickerbocker News*

In expressing our appreciation of the relationship which we have enjoyed with you and the hope that you will avail yourself of any of the bank's complete line of services, may we remind you that the adoption of the bank's new name requires no action on your part—JUST CONTINUE TO USE YOUR PRESENT CHECKS AND OTHER FORMS UNTIL EXHAUSTED.

New York (N.Y.) *Times*

Management should plan in advance for restraining persons displaced by automation.

New York (N.Y.) *Journal of Commerce*

She has two famous brothers and seven half-sisters noted for their abundant production of milk.

Chicago (Ill.) *Tribune*

A new loudspeaker system has been installed in the church. It was given by one of the members in memory of his wife.

Lansing (Mich.) *Christian Banner*

The High School Junior class members are busy working on the class play, "Ready Made Family," which they plan to produce in the near future.

St. Paul (Nebr.) *Phonograph*

Dave is the younger brother of the Phil's ace, Dennis Bennett. The 19-year-old righthanded curveballer is just 18 years old!

Philadelphia (Pa.) *Inquirer*

The competition, beginning at 8 p. m. will have contests for 12 corps comprised of three senior corps, five junior units and four pee-pee units.

Fort Smith (Ark.) *Southwest American*

Harmony Park Ballroom asked a permit to operate under the newd dance ordinance.

Santa Ana (Calif.) *Register*

Edward Hillston broke his arm at the party last week. It was a decided success and many express a wish that it might be an annual affair.

Hillsboro (Wisc.) *Sentry-Enterprise*

A freight engine darted off ice-clogged rails at Glenwood, Missouri. The brakeman was kissed as he jumped from the window.

Boston (Mass.) *Record American*

Several hours passed before the plane was missed, although it had cracked up barely two minutes before takeoff.

Bethlehem (Pa.) *Globe-Times*

Abraham Lincoln was born in a house which he helped his father to build.

Bainbridge (N.Y.) *News*

Williams told the Welfare Director that his house and wife were full of kids.

Fort Smith (Ark.) *News*

Never break your bread or roll in your soup.

Nashville (Tenn.) *Tennessean*

WEATHER FORECAST: Light, moderate east-westerly winds, fair tonight and Tuesday, becoming cooler and a little warmer.

Niagara Falls (Canada) *Evening Review*

They received a large number of valuable parents from their friends.

El Paso (Tex.) *Herald*

Miss Ruth Mitchell was injured at the farm of her grandfather, Whitney Dean, Thursday by being ignored by a cow.

New York (N.Y.) *Times*

A good attendance was present Sunday A. M. Reverend Alex W. Nichols has been sent to another district.

Murfreesboro (Tenn.) *Daily News Journal*

Dean S. P. Swenson came through sensationally in his high school talk, packing as smartly-contrived a 10-minute speech into 20 minutes as this town has recently heard.

Pullman (Wash.) *Herald*

The couple have found an apartment in Berkeley where they will live until after their marriage until the future benedict receives his degree from UC in June.

San Francisco (Calif.) *Examiner*

The Peace Corps soon will begin a pilot senior-year program, providing sex weeks of summer training for 500 to 700 college juniors who have applied for the corps.

Seattle (Wash.) *Daily Times*

The Dodgers' quartet selected in the annual poll of members of the Baseball Writers Assn. include shortstop Maury Wills, outfielder Tommy Davis, left-handed pitcher Sandy Koufax and eight-handed pitcher Don Drysdale.

Orlando (Fla.) *Sentinel*

Especially well received was the duet sung by Mrs. Morrison and Mrs. Wilkerson, with the former disguised as a lady.

Pompton Lakes (N.J.) *Ledger*

A lifeboat was thrown to the girl, and this she managed to grasp at the second attempt.

Detroit (Mich.) *Free Press*

Two men narrowly escaped death yesterday afternoon on Lake Michigan as their boat overturned after hitting a tug boat. The only thing that kept them from drowning was the fact that they were not in the boat, but having a beer at Mike's Tavern which is located about 50 yards from the lake.

Cleveland (Ohio) *Plain Dealer*

The dog failed to recognize Montclair as his owner after the barber had removed his whiskers and bit him in the leg.

Newark (N.J.) *Evening News*

A beginning reporter for the Santa Ana (Calif.) *Register* learned to never write notes to his editor on news copy after this sentence made print in his story on a gas explosion: "The apartment filled with the deadly cooking gas (strike deadly if you don't want to offend Southern Counties Gas Co.)."

Santa Ana (Calif.) *Register*

Born to Mr. and Mrs. Ben Pitts, a little daughter Earlie.

Chicago (Ill.) *Tribune*

Then add one pound of candied pineapple. Bake in pans that have cans and one pound of Brazil nuts in shells. Bake in pants that have been lined with brown paper and buttered.

El Paso (Tex.) *Herald-Post*

Mr. and Mrs. Warren Hopewell will go to housekeeping on Elm Road. They have many friends to extend good dishes.

Warren (Ohio) *Tribune Chronicle*

At the reception following the wedding, the captivating bride in her low cut wedding gown, was easily the "belly of the ball."

Atlanta (Ga.) *Constitution*

Mr. Smith, now 78 years old, cultivated his 118 acre farm, milking crows and raising turkeys.

Sherman (Tex.) *Democrat*

Big cattle show at Tolchester Beach. Go over, see the show and meet your friends.

Baltimore (Md.) *Sun*

EASTER WEATHER FORECAST: Cloudy, with occasional flowers.

Van Buren (Ark.) *Press-Argus*

Jim Wilkins was painfully injured when a widow was blown out of the church during the evening's services.

Wilmington (N.C.) *News*

Mrs. Florence Sunderman, president, presided and opened the meeting with a poem, and the Lord's Prayer was read and approved.

Huntington (Ind.) *Herald-Press*

Lieutenant Kennedy helped work his way through Northwestern University by acting as a motorcycle in Evanston.

New York (N.Y.) *Daily Mirror*

The East Franklin Board of Education lessened its teacher shortage problem by firing three new teachers at a recent meeting.

Akron (Ohio) Beacon Journal

Judging of the essays will be based partly on spelling, punctuation and grammaticak correctness.

Wildwood (N.J.) Leader

He scored with one out on a single by O'Connell, and the latter took second on the Needless throw to the plate. Aaron singled for the third time to score O'Connell. Another Needless throw to the plate put Aaron on second.

Chicago (Ill.) Tribune

The ball struck Berra on the right temple and knocked him cold. He was taken to Ford Hospital. X-ray pictures of Berra's head showed nothing.

New York (N.Y.) Herald Tribune

As we look down, we see a mass of faces on the floor, dancing arm in arm.

Cleveland (Ohio) Press

Those who witnessed the freak of nature said that this swirling hurricane extended 3,000 feet in the air and covered a large area as it swept in from the lake to be finally dissipated after it had picked up hundreds of chickens, carrying them into the air and removing most of their fathers before dropping them into the chicken yard.

Erie (Pa.) News

William Holton lost a finger when a poisoned dog to which he was administering an anecdote bit him.

El Paso (Tex.) *Herald-Post*

Mr. and Mrs. Frank Di Petro, of Miles Avenue, are receiving congratulations on the birth of a daughter. Both mother and baby are doing nicely under the car of Dr. Robert Sievers.

Bordentown (N.J.) *Register*

Watch out for the pancake supper sponsored by the Mikana Ladies Aid.

Rice Lake (Wisc.) *Chronotype*

When finished cooking, top with a meringue made by combining 2 beaten egg whites with ¼ cup sugar and 1 tablespoonful candied finger (finely chopped).

Chicago (Ill.) *News*

A beautiful luncheon complimented the muchly feeted bride-elect.

Bradenton (Fla.) *Herald*

Following the ceremony, a wedding supper was hell at the home.

Pittsburgh (Kan.) *Headlight*

Miss Sarah Durham of New Salem complained thieves killed a calf in a pasture and dragged it to her father's barn where they butchered it, for the second time within the last few weeks.

Brownsville (Pa.) *Telegraph*

The high wind damaged the schoolhouse and injured the teacher. Miss Wilma May Kraft had a gable end blown off and was moved six inches on her foundation.

Muskogee (Okla.) *Phoenix*

We are very happy to have as our guest preacher this morning one other than our Pastor Emeritus, Rev. Leon H. Austin.

Coventry (Conn.) *Church Bulletin*

The mayor said that unless added revenue was forthcoming, several teachers indicated they plan to leave their pests.

Philadelphia (Pa.) *Inquirer*

Four men whom Larry MacPhail characterizes as the greatest minds in modern baseball have become a sort of unofficial board of strategy for the pilot of the Cincinnati Reds in his efforts to build up his team for the 1934 season. The quartet is composed of Branch and Rogers Hornsby.

Savannah (Ga.) *News*

Asked if "Dizzy" gave any reason for his sudden decision to give up his holdout tactics, Breadon said, " 'Diz' simply said that he had changed his wind."

New Orleans (La.) *Times-Picayune*

Worried about the screaming nervous breakdowns that pass for popular sons these days?

Chattanooga (Tenn.) *News-Free Press*

101

About 465 members of the staff, their wives and sweethearts attended the annual dance.

Columbus (Ohio) *Citizen-Journal*

Smith was practicing landing off Newport News, Virginia, in an observation seaplane when a wing dipped into the surface of the water. He was catapulted from the craft some thirty feet and began to sing.

Columbus (Ind.) *Republican*

There was no need to apply artificial respiration because Murrin voluntarily resumed consciousness.

Detroit (Mich.) *Edison Synchroscope*

Oliver Wendell Holmes had three children, all of whom lived to maternity.

Waco (Tex.) *Times-Herald*

The house and barn were swept away by the wind. I had several mules in the barn, but they tell me they didn't get hurt.

Memphis (Tenn.) *Commercial Appeal*

Plan to eat dinner on November 3rd with the Baptist ladies. The same wonderful dinner as they served on election day.

Custer County (Nebr.) *Chief*

Following the ceremony there was an informal reaction in the vestibule of the church.

Newport (Ark.) *Daily Independent*

A second group of immigrants from Okinawa is expected to arrive by the end of September. They will be instructed in breeding and will be equipped with all things necessary to start their new life.

New York (N.Y.) *Times*

Eugene D. Fletchall, manager of Swift & Co.'s South San Francisco packing plant, has been elected a vice president and will be quartered in Chicago.

San Francisco (Calif.) *News*

Simon Shields lost a horse the first of the week that he valued very highly. It was the one he went to housekeeping with.

South Bend (Ind.) *Mishawaka Tribune*

Mrs. Sarah Putnam is poorly this spring—her face is much missed in church, it being always there when she is able to be present.

Woodstock (Vt.) *Vermont Standard*

Mr. Sheppard quotes an old lady as saying: "I don't want the visitor from the church coming around saving her soul on me."

Greenville (S.C.) *Church Bulletin*

" 'I's very happy,' said Olga, a medical student, in perfect English."

Lynchburg (Va.) *Daily Advance*

Speaking of Pratt School, the PTA there is busily organizing the annual Pratt Fall Festival.

Minneapolis (Minn.) *Star*

This happened in the third when Detore got the first Brewer hit, a single to left. Then, in winding up, Stout's arm hit his leg and rolled away for a balk.

Columbus (Ohio) *Citizen Journal*

In three days Chilean-born ballerina Lupe Serrano learned a role that takes three weeks to learn and got the American Ballet Theater out of a tights squeeze.

Dayton (Ohio) *News*

There he was, swimming in the cold water, Battling heroically against the waves. "Just a half-mile more," he thought, "and I'll make the shore." His strokes were getting weaker. He could hardly lift an arm any more. The beach was only a few yards away. His last efforts were too much. He began to grow dizzy. Then his head began to swim and carried him to the shore.

Philadelphia (Pa.) *Bulletin*

As Mr. and Mrs. Horace M. Wardley were walking home from the dance, a large dog attacked them and bit Mr. Wardley on the public square.

Stockton (Calif.) *Record*

The house was trimmed in pink, white and blue with babies hanging from the ceiling and nursing bottles galore.

Bellows Falls (Vt.) *Times*

He remarked in all seriousness that it was hereditary in his family to have no children.

St. Louis (Mo.) *Post-Dispatch*

Murphy took a couple of shots at the posse, jumped on his horse and rode off in all directions.
St. Louis (Mo.) *Post-Dispatch*

Dial A Prayer . . . You have done it before but try again. The suggestion may be given by a friend and you may dismiss it with a sigh . . . wondering what a new prayer can do for you. Such an instance happened to me and I dialed 374-2365 and a voice said: "Hell, I am Ralph Rhea, minister of Unity Center of Miami."
Miami Beach (Fla.) *Daily Sun*

Mr. Haines has sad 12 years teaching experience.
Canton (Ohio) Glenwood High School
Eagle's View

Alpha Mu has been busy making plans for their dance. Boys, you'd better pet your dates now.
Fayetteville (N.Y.) *Eagle-Bulletin*

The All-Girl orchestra was rather weak in the bras section.
Kingsport (Tenn.) *Times*

Mrs. Stanley Chopin served the guests chicken with muchroom on toast.
Phoenix (Ariz.) *Republic*

We've had so many inquiries concerning barbecues that we're sure this delightful form of entertaining is coming into its own. It certainly has everything in its favor. For those who don't enjoy messing with a fire there are the charcoal broilers, which can be purchased ready to set up, or the foundation can be built of brick or stones with a grate for the charcoal and girls above the grate.

Los Angeles (Calif.) *Herald-Examiner*

Sixty-five participated in the Lions' outing at Swing Flats last evening, and enjoyed a bounteous feed, including a half of a spring chicken deliciously fried.

Tooele (Utah) *Bulletin*

Later, four-breasted girls danced for the evangelist and his party.

(New York, N.Y.) Associated Press

I will still act in the capacity of Peace Officer, and will be glad to serve any civil papers, and anyone wishing to be arrested for violating any of the State laws, their patronage will be appreciated also.

Mena (Ark.) *Star*

George O. Sanford, engineer in the Department of the Interior, will deliver an illustrated lecture on "The Construction of the Hoover Dame." The public is invited.

Washington (D.C.) *Evening Star*

Because this new law had created a hardship in practically every community in the state, it is expected that it will be repeated next year, it was reported here.

Marquette (Mich.) *Mining Journal*

Lynne was shaken up when her mount balked at the second obstacle and she was thrown, striking the rail and coming to rest on the fat side.

Burlington (Vt.) *Free Press*

Messrs. Harrington and Thompson suffered badly frozen feet, due to wearing oxfords, frosted ears and fingers.

Minot (N.D.) *News*

A nudist wife is just like any other wife about clothes. She wants a wink coat just as much as any other woman.

Muncie (Ind.) *Star*

Michael Arlen lunched with Alice Terry in a black hat.

Los Angeles (Calif.) *Herald-Examiner*

Fortunately for the deceased, he had deposited all of his money in the bank the day before, so he lost virtually nothing but his life.

Philadelphia (Pa.) *Inquirer*

Many renters keep pictures of loved ones who have died in the bank boxes.

Fort Worth (Tex.) *Press*

The central figure in the investigation, bond broker and speculator pleaded guilty to 31 counts of forging and uttering sssssssssssssssssssss and now is under sentence of 31 to 635 years in the State penitentiary.

Pine Bluff (Ark.) *Commercial*

He has been in the Army 12 years and has risen to the rant of sergeant.

(New York, N.Y.) Associated Press

The subcommittee is also investigating charges that servicemen are used to perform mental tasks for officers.

St. Louis (Mo.) *Post-Dispatch*

Pour water and butter on the front part of the stove, as soon as it comes to a boil, add all of the flour and stir vigorously.

Newburgh (N.Y.) *Beacon News*

Lloyd George, former Prime Minister of England was about to address a church group as his chairman said to the enthusiastic audience: "Friends, we all know that the Bishop of ———— is a terrible liar, but thank God, we have a match for him on the platform tonight."

Chicago (Ill.) *Christian Advocate*

State highway patrolmen have been assigned to aid in holding up motorists.

Seattle (Wash.) *Star*

Vincent Youngman was arrested Saturday by Evanston police on a charge of drinking while intoxicated.

Evanston (Ill.) *Review*

Clothes hangers and shoe trees increase the life of their wearers.

Denver (Colo.) News-Times

Among the Eskimos it is an unwritten law that if any man, from any cause whatsoever, slaps his neighbor, the wife and family of the deceased must be cared for by the slayer during the rest of their lives.

Bangor (Me.) News

After the operation he failed to rally, lapsing into a comma from which he never fully emerged.

Chicago (Ill.) Tribune

He was sentenced to five years in district court, on a bigamy charge.

Hutchinson (Kan.) News

Lt. Jimmie E. Gibson, wife and baby left Sunday for Hawaii, where they will be stationed for three years. Friends here hope they will like their trip and stay in the islands.

Marble Falls (Tex.) Messenger

Suppose your child, 3, dislikes peas. Don't put a spoonful of peas on his plate or try to push a big portion of them into him. Put two or three peas on his plate, with nothing else. Don't tell him he must eat them. Just say he can't have any other food unless he does.

El Paso (Tex.) Times

In the kitchen she put on water for a few sand-wiches.

New York (N.Y.) *News*

After seeing an opera based on a story from the Bible, a reviewer wrote: "The only signs of the bibical story were the fatted calves."

Boston (Mass.) *Globe*

Kingstate visit to Italy. They will have and Queen Frederika of Greece private audience with Pope ar-rived today for a three-day John.

New York (N.Y.) *Daily Mirror*

Without saying another word, she pulled the pistol from her handbag and shot her husband three times in the attic.

Louisville (Ky.) *Times*

A score of informal cocktail parties had preceded the Press Club dinner. An improper supper party was to follow it.

Washington (D.C.) *Post*

One desiring to vote a straight Republican ticket will place an X in the circle at the top of the ballot before the party name "DEMOCRATIC."

Mattoon (Ill.) *Journal-Gazette*

The Chamber of Commerce held their wide awake monthly meeting Tuesday night. Twenty-five members were present. The President was marooned in Ridgeway on account of flood conditions. While his vacant face was missed the chair was adequately filled by the Vice-president.

Ridgeway (Pa.) *Record*

Mrs. Flores had lived at the sanitarium since 1959 when she suffered a hip fracture, in which she encountered landing gear trouble which cut her air speed considerably.

San Bernardino (Calif.) *Sun-Telegram*

Mrs. Edwin Evans had the misfortune of having her head cut by falling on the ice, which bled profusely.

Meadville (Pa.) *Tribune*

Mr. McCord became worse and it was discovered that he was suffering from members of his family.

Atlanta (Ga.) *Constitution*

"Worry not only accomplishes nothing, but it kills more people than old age does," says Harriet Howarth, who has just celebrated her 4th birthday.

New York (N.Y.) *Daily Mirror*

Two of the most glamorous ladies they saw were the baritone's wife, whose gown shimmered solidly with 24-photographers on the inside.

Kansas City (Mo). *Times*

If you are not fortunate enough to have one of these modern ranges, preheat the oven to 450 degrees and place the foot in it, it will be ready to serve in one hour.

Los Angeles (Calif.) *Times*

The millinery department will be on the second floor and the proprietor states that their aim will be to always have the latest and last word in women's hats at appalling prices.

Union City (Ind.) *Times*

The Floritans nudist camp will hold a Halloween party this week-end when 500 persons attend a convention there, but no costumes will be permitted.

Delray (Fla.) *News-Journal*

In 1900 he began an association that lasted practically uninterrupted until his death when he became head clerk of the Windsor hotel.

Denver (Colo.) *Rocky Mountain News*

He told it well—it had been funny when it happened, and it was still funny, to Father as well. I hadn't heard him laugh so heartily since Mother died.

(New York, N.Y.) *True Confessions*

Court records show that he was acquitted of using an automobile without its permission.

Polk County (Tenn.) *Record*

A Jolly cab-driver was convicted Saturday of putting oil of mustard on the seat of a Yellow Cab in City Court.

Memphis (Tenn.) *Press-Scimitar*

As soon as an application is received at Army head-quarters, the board will look over past military records, and finally the applicant will be called in for an interview. Then the board makes up its mind and sends the dope to Washington.

Albany (N.Y.) *Knickerbocker News*

If you use lemon juice, squeeze it from fresh oranges.

Philadelphia (Pa.) *Inquirer*

Women teachers must also stipulate that they "will not go out with any young man except insofar as it may be necessary to stimulate Sunday School work." This restriction is said to allow a great deal of lassitude.

Charlotte (N.C.) *News*

On Saturday night, he concluded, 242 persons, not intoxicated but dead drunk, were taken to the police station.

New York (N.Y.) *Times*

Although she made no statement on the elimination of her seat, sources said she was caught by surprise.

Harrisburg (Pa.) *Evening News*

A nine-year-old girl broke her left arm yesterday when she fell from a tree. Wanda Todd, 1 Rogers

St., was taken to Professional Center Hospital after a temporary splint was placed on her leg by ambulance attendants.

Montgomery (Ala.) *Advertiser*

Mr. Ringling eats sparingly; smokes denicotinized cigars, takes daily exercises and until the beginning of this illness was able to touch the floor with his finger tips without bending.

New York (N.Y.) *World-Telegram*

The rise in sales of nylons was in addition to substantial sales of stockings in the form of the popular stretch tights, for which adequate figures have not yet been completed.

New York (N.Y.) *Times*

James Creekmore died Saturday night after a fight of many weeks in the arms of his brother.

Nashville (Tenn.) *Banner*

Rudd denied that he had threatened to get them back because he had been double-crossed. Defense council branded Rudd as "a self-admitted thief, a liar, and a guitar player."

Durham (N.C.) *Herald*

The slightly built general, with four rows of robbins on his chest, took the witness chair.

Greensboro (N.C.) *Record*

Mrs. Wilkins had the bee trapped under her skirt. While attempting to dislodge it the bee stung her you know what.

Muncie (Ind.) *Press*

He looked across at her, sitting on a cushion before the fire, her chin resting on her knees, her eyes clasped about them. Something elusive, ethereal to her, he felt . . . and he knew he could not do it.

Baltimore (Md.) *Sunday American*

With his free hand he raised his hat, bent his head and kissed her on the forehead.

Des Moines (Iowa) *Register*

Young men are doing their own choosing these days, and a good way to scare them away, they admit, is to look expectant.

San Antonio (Tex.) *News*

The Teen Club will hold a hayride tomorrow evening. Members are reminded to bring blankets as hay is not available.

Sandia Base (N.M.) *Crossroads*

Instead of going to the bridge party Thursday evening, Mrs. Moore stayed home and entertained her husband.

Van Buren (Ark.) *Press Argus*

The girl went to the forward ladies' room.

New York (N.Y.) *Herald Tribune*

Since it requires eight percent more energy to stand than sit, the wide homemaker does as much of her work in a sitting position as possible.

North Platte (Nebr.) *Telegraph-Bulletin*

Mrs. Fultz spoke of the increasing number of men's garden clubs in Florida and noted the special ability men have in propagation.

Orlando (Fla.) *Sentinel*

The program was given by Mrs. William Elmer, who presented a lesson on 'Hot Beds' and 'Cold Frames' which was very interesting.

Gunnison (Colo.) *News-Champion*

Movie announcement: "The Fly," which visited Detroit last summer, soon to return to the screen.

Detroit (Mich.) *News*

The unfortunate woman was killed while cooking her husband's breakfast in a horrible manner.

Cincinnati (Ohio) *Enquirer*

Her father was formerly minister of war of the republic of Venezuela. She is 32. Her husband is two years old, a magazine writer.

Greensburg (Pa.) *Morning Review*

Lipstick, rouge and powder are all that good taste requires for street wear.

Rochester (N.Y.) *Democrat and Chronicle*

As usual, there was a representative crowd in attendance at the musical tea sponsored by Strains' tea room. The program was interesting and varied and women of the city welcomed an opportunity to gather for a catty hour over the tea cups.

Great Falls (Mont.) *Tribune*

Mrs. Nelson was presented with a gift from the chapter in appreciation of work well done by Mrs. Ethel Abramson.

Houston (Minn.) *Signal*

There are millions of desirable women who are unattacked and hungry for love.

Omaha (Nebr.) *Shopping Guide*

There was a surprise birthday party given Wednesday night for Mrs. Beavens. Much credit is given to Mr. Beavens for being able to keep Mrs. Beavens at home.

Nashville (Tenn.) *Banner*

To remove a fresh grease spot on a rug, cover the spot with blotting paper, then press with a hot flatiron. Cover the spot with magnesia, let it remain for 24 years, then brush off.

San Bernardino (Calif.) *Daily Sun*

To make a delicious rabbit stew, use four diced carrots, one large onion, six medium sized potatoes and one large hair.

Tucson (Ariz.) *Citizen*

Mrs. Williams of the Home Garden Club, gave a short talk on how to keep ants out of your blooming pants.

Muskogee (Okla.) *Times-Democrat*

The first large floor will seat 600 persons, then there is a double gallery that will seat an additional number of people with upholstered seats.

Macon (Ga.) *Telegraph*

There has been a strong undercurrent of resentment against Mr. Armstrong-Jones who, at 30, and the top of a successful career as a photographer, has sown a few wild cats in his time.

New York (N.Y.) *Herald Tribune*

President Coolidge had for breakfast, on Friday, with griddle cakes and sausages, Borah of Idaho, Walsh of Montana, Curtis of Kansas City, and Watson of Indiana.

Pittsburgh (Pa.) *Sunday Post*

Could you possibly print an exercise in your column which will develop my things to make them larger?

New Orleans (La.) *Times-Picayune*

Miss Barbara Nickerson attributes her beauty to the fact that she once decided to "be sensible" in her daily habits. "Be sensible and don't ever indulge in your daily habits," she advised today.

Boston (Mass.) *Globe*

At the May meeting of the Greenville Home Demonstration Club, Mrs. C. C. Hedrick read a poem and gave a review of the book, 'Naked Came I' by David Weiss. Mrs. O. S. Mann and Mrs. J. R. Johnson gave demonstrations.

Monroe (W.Va.) *Watchman-Union*

Harry M. Wootten, consultant to the tobacco industry, smoked an estimated 369 billion cigarettes in the year ending at midnight Dec. 31, a drop of 25 million smokes.

Mamaroneck (N.Y.) *Times*

He spent his time in making hooked rugs, cooking friends and relatives.

Rochester (N.Y.) *Times-Union*

While he may be poor and shabby, underneath those ragged trousers beats a heart of gold.

Boston (Mass.) *Globe*

Men are not permitted to enter the ladies' bath. The male bath attendant under paragraph eight of the bath regulations is to be regarded as a woman.

St. Louis (Mo.) *Post-Dispatch*

Mrs. Winston Churchill told members of the YWCA committees in Liverpool: "Ninety percent of the mistresses on YWCA hostel beds are not fit to sleep on."

London (England) *Daily Express*

We single girls drive our own cars, support our own children, go and come as we wish.

Los Angeles (Calif.) *Mirror*

Reservations may be made for ladies in boxes only.

New York (N.Y.) *Times*

The Junior Ladies Aid will serve an oyster at the church Saturday evening.

Indianola (Iowa) *Record-Herald & Tribune*

The entire program given by the visiting club was greatly enjoyed. Mrs. Vivian Phillips, a night club song girl, was shot to death. Refreshments were served by the hostesses.

Monticello (Ind.) *Herald-Journal*

Mr. and Mrs. Arthur G. McKay and daughter Leona held Open House on Friday for their few friends.

Fairview Park (Ohio) *Herald*

To clean a white fur coat, remove all trimmings and rub in plenty of white cornmeal with the hands, then beat the hat with a yardstick.

Pasadena (Calif.) *Independent*

In making Swiss steak, add the salt and pepper to the floor before pounding it into the meat.

Hartford (Conn.) *Daily Courant*

Mrs. Harry B. Ireland's display won the Harry B. Ireland trophy as best original or asiatic garden.

Santa Barbara (Calif.) *News-Press*

Rita Hayworth said yesterday that she was flat busted and that she felt sorry for her husband, Dick Haymes, who has worries of his own.

Los Angeles (Calif.) *Daily News*

Queen Elizabeth arrived to begin a Paris visit that inspired the warmest welcome the French have given any royal figure since they guillotined their own Queen Marie Antoinette.

(New York, N.Y.) United Press

If you happen to sit on the floor to put on shoes and stockings, do a flop, lift eggs in air, wiggle the toes.

San Francisco (Calif.) *Call Bulletin*

We could go on indefinitely about the graces of hundreds of charming matrons in this town, all growing lovier with time.

Blackfoot (Idaho) *Bulletin*

Should the middle-aged avoid using soup on the face?

Little Rock (Ark.) *Arkansas Gazette*

The salad should be made from an alligator pear, sliced tomatoes, water cress and a dash of mayonnaise. Serve with a tart French waitress.

Spokane (Wash.) *Press*

She made the statement as she received the Woman of the Rear Award.

New York (N.Y.) *Daily News*

Mr. Brown has grown in stature through the ears.

El Paso (Tex.) *Times*

The old excuse that 'nice guys' are hard to find is unmitigated malarkey. Boston has hordes of them. The reason you are still single is because you haven't exposed yourself in the right places.

Boston (Mass.) *Post*

Party in which Miss Edith Spear makes her bow to society in New York with dinner and supper dance, will cost approximately $50,000. Expenses include special rain for guests from Philadelphia.

Philadelphia (Pa.) *Inquirer*

Picking up the living-room before going to bed takes only five minutes, but is worth a half hour in the morning.

Spokane (Wash.) *Chronicle*

This cream-cheese decoration for open-faced pies tastes as dreary as it looks.

New York (N.Y.) *World-Telegram*

A horse belonging to Jed Applegate died last night from a strange melody.

Macon (Ga.) *News*

The expected starters are Don Drysdale from the Dodgers and Camilo Pascual from the Twins. Drysdale will be pitching with only three days rest between tarts.

Long Island (N.Y.) *Newsday*

Blankets were at a premium today because of the chilly blasts that swept Wrigley Field. Many wrapped their legs up with newspapers and then tossed them on the field and seats as park attendants frowned.

Chicago (Ill.) *Defender*

John Howard, 103 years old, died Monday of what was thought to be old age.

Cleveland (Ohio) *Press*

She replaces the Rev. Marshal Lamar Smith, pastor of the Quitman Presbyterian Church, who found the pressure of pastoral duties too heavy to permit his carrying on in the classroom.

Quitman (Ga.) *Free Press*

The bride's table was laid with white lace over pink, centered with an anniversary candle surrounded with bouquets of brides attendants.

Borger (Tex.) *News-Herald*

The sudden cyclone destroyed the house and three children are missing. Neighbors donated a bed to give the couple a new start.

Springfield (Mo.) *Leader & Press*

Bill Schraft is reported as being confined to his home by illness. His man friends are hoping for his speedy recovery.

Tampa (Fla.) *Tribune*

Mrs. Florence Miles is the proud mother of a fine 8 pound boy. Her mother-in-law and husband have returned to St. Louis after the visit to see the wife and baby.

Sedalia (Mo.) *Democrat*

John Garberick, 18, was found guilty of assaulting Larry Mollenkopf, 16, during an argument with a package of frozen fish.

Jackson (Miss.) *News*

"The death of the patient terminates the physician-patient relationship."

(Columbus, Ohio) *State Medical Journal*

Tom Mix and his wonder horse, Tony, are featured this week in "The Yankee Señor." Tom shows careful training in some of the stunts, in which he exercises almost human intelligence.

Dallas (Tex.) *Times Herald*

It will be Bermuda shorts and grilled hamburgers in the back yard at the party Miss Wilkins is giving.

Chicago (Ill.) *Tribune*

GAMES SUNDAY:
Brooklyn at Milwaukee
New York at St. Louis (2)
Pittsburgh at Chicago (2)
Philharmonic at Cincinnati (2)

New York (N.Y.) *World-Telegram & Sun*

Karl Marx was a descendant of a long line of rabbits, but the whole family embraced Christianity when Karl was in his sixth year.

Greenfield (Mass.) *Recorder-Gazette*

Before they reached the license bureau, the bride-and-bridegroom-to-be skidded off the road into a cuddle.

Elwood (Ill.) *Ledger*

Friends of Mr. and Mrs. Fred Jones will be relieved to learn that she and Mr. Frank McKinney who live in Miami, Florida, were injured in the recent hurricane.

Denver (Colo.) *Post*

T. J. Jennings has recovered from an attack of hiccoughs which lasted ten days and nights. The hiccoughs left as aburptly as they came.

Harrisonburg (Va.) *Daily News-Record*

Mrs. Sarah Firestone has returned to her home after having been confined at the bedside of her daughter.

St. Louis (Mo.) *Post-Dispatch*

It has a little street of shops and iron lacework with homemade bread.

Chicago (Ill.) *Daily Tribune*

Before the verdict was rendered this morning 'Miss Mexico' told interviewers that if the court freed her, she would become a nut.

Chicago (Ill.) *Daily Tribune*

Police Chief A. O. Lower, who also was in the courtroom, offered to cooperate 10 percent in battling prostitution and said he would issue orders accordingly to the police department.

Canton (Ohio) *Repository*

Statistics show that 86 percent have left because of ill-health, death, marriage or other disasters which could occur to most anyone.

New York (N.Y.) *Times*

Breeding stock, and in later years, seamen, have gone to Japan, Italy, Portugal, Germany, Australia, all the Latin American countries and many others.

Milwaukee (Wisc.) *Journal*

The Ken Maynard horse is Tarzan. He is married to a non-professional.

Boston (Mass.) *Traveler*

And the first thing he did was to rescue Lucy Grant's dog and promptly fall in love with her.

(New York, N.Y.) *American Magazine*

126

The Giants let Pittsburgh get two runs in the first inning and then finished up by trimming them 3 to 0.

New York (N.Y.) *Telegraph*

The pulpit may be as faultless in its presentation of ethics as it is admired for its beautiful ritual, but it will never touch the hearts or shape the livers of men who toil.

Lexington (N.C.) *Dispatch*

MARRIAGE LICENSES ISSUED

Anna M. Grimes, 3825 Terrace St., and
Ernest F. Snyder, 3366 Frederick St.
Anna M. Grimes, 3825 Terrace St., and
Erward Dunston, 8712 Laycock Ave.

Philadelphia (Pa.) *Inquirer*

The tropical hurricane which virtually demolished Santo Domingo several years ago turned up along the North Carolina coast today, with revived strength.

Toronto (Canada) *Daily Star*

Boil one quart of water until tender.

Wilkes-Barre (Pa.) *Record*

The latest news is that Wilma Simpkins is in bed and desires that all friends call.

McComb (Miss.) *Enterprise-Journal*

A son was born to Mr. and Mrs. William Kleintop, Lehigh Avenue, during the past week. Congratulations, Pete!

Palmerton (Pa.) *Press*

Hogan contended evidence by the Government in the trial court failed to show any connection whatso-ever between the contract and the loan, made between old friends who have slept out under the stars together, upon a promissory note.

Los Angeles (Calif.) *Times*

It was learned that Mrs. Cora Bennett, one of our members, had departed to join Mr. Bennett in another world at two-thirty Wednesday.

St. Louis (Mo.) *Globe-Democrat*

An unemployed electrician died of a heart attack while huntin gin the rugged mountains near here Saturday.

Chattanooga (Tenn.) *Times*

Unpleasant smoke that sometimes arises when cooking hot cakes can be avoided by tying some salt in a bag and rubbing the girdle with this instead of greasing it.

Charlotte (N.C.) *News*

A veterinary fixed the paw and for the present he goes on three legs.

Worcester (Mass.) *Evening Gazette*

Bob Gibson, who reported yesterday, will not be able to itch for several days.

Washington (D.C.) *Star*

They worked with an ax in one hand, and a gun in the other, and a Bible in the other.

Atlanta (Ga.) *Church Bulletin*

Dianne's wedding drew a terrific crowd, including coy Sally B., whom we thought was a broad.

Hollywood (Calif.) *Dots and Dashes*

The storm is due to strike this section before tomorrow morning, unless postponed on account of the weather.

Catskill (N.Y.) *Daily World*

The passengers had stampeded to the port rail in fear of wind and wives.

Pensacola (Fla.) *News*

All last winter he slept in a bed with his lower extremities perched ten inches above his head, to hoist up a sagging stomach.

New York (N.Y.) *Evening World*

Miss Florence Shipley and Herman Jones were wed at the Court House before proceeding to the hospital. Mrs. Jones is now the proud mother of a bouncing boy.

Van Buren (Ark.) *Press Argus*

PRESS BONERS

He was given 10 days in jail for hurling rocks at a school official's residence and pouring syrup on his ear.

Hereford (Tex.) *Sunday Brand*

If you burn toast, and most of us do sometimes, then push it up and down very lightly on your garter.

San Antonio (Tex.) *Express-News*

If the present trend continues at least one out of every white men born in the United States probably will die of heart disease.

Brunswick (Ga.) *News*

NOTICE TO DOG OWNERS: I am about to return assessor's books to Mt. Pleasant township, and those that have dogs without tags on will be shot.

W. J. Crump, Assessor.

Whiteside (Ill.) *Sentinel*

Every seat in the grandstand and bleachers was filled. No seats were obtainable after 9:30 o'clock in the morning. Hundreds of persons were turned down for seats.

Pueblo (Colo.) *Star-Journal*

The pastor reports 26 funerals, 17 weddings, and 9 baptisms during the year just ended. The year has been a good one, with many causes for rejoicing.

Alameda (Calif.) *Church Bulletin*

Several churches have beautiful religious scenes depicting the birth of Christ on their front lawns.

El Paso (Tex.) *Herald-Post*

Lord Northesk will be Peggy's fifth husband. In her matrimonial ventures she has been a countess but she never has been a lady.

Syracuse (N.Y.) *Journal*

Blizzard-like weather moved in from the southwest along about midnight last night, and those who sleep light said there were high guests starting about midnight and reaching a peak around 2 o'clock this morning.

Monmouth (Ill.) *Review Atlas*

Bill Rogers, Richmond, has a 'trick' right knee that goes out of joint and leaves his knee stiff. He is a dancer.

Johnny Filipeck, Chicago, reported abrasions of the left knee. He was the thrill driver on Monday night who jumped his car over a bus and one of the drivers in a head-on crash.

Both were sympathized with at the Allentown hospital dispensary.

Allentown (Pa.) *Morning Call*

Germans are so small that there may be as many as one billion, seven hundred million of them in a drop of water.

Mobile (Ala.) *Press*

Mr. and Mrs. Benny Croset announce the birth of a little son which arrived on the 5:15 last Thursday.

West Union (Ohio) *People's Defender*

Prosecutor Charles S. Bell and Assistant Prosecutor Louis Schneider, representing the State, asked all prospective jurors if they would inflict the death penalty "if the evidence warranted it." Those who said they were opposed to capital punishment under any circumstances were executed.

Cincinnati (Ohio) *Times-Star*

He suffered a slight stroke about one month ago and never recovered until his death.

New Kensington (Pa.) *Daily Dispatch*

ROQUEFORT SALAD DRESSING

1 cup Roquefort cheese

An hour of real companionship does more to insure a fine parent-child relationship than many hours of bored association.

1 tablespoon Worcestershire sauce

Boston (Mass.) *Globe*

It is scandalous to see these Society women going about with a poodle dog on the end of a string where a baby would be more fitting.

Chicago (Ill.) *News*

The game will begin at 7 P. M. and is to be played with the aid of moonshine and electric lights.

Boston (Mass.) *Globe*

Rev. Williams stated that David had only one fault, a slight tendency to adultery.

Charleston (W.Va) *Mail*

The marriage was a very quiet affair and was un-attended by bridesmaids or bridegrooms.

St. Louis (Mo.) *Post-Dispatch*

The mainland prepared for the season's first big blow as President Truman arrived for a speech to veterans.

Miami (Fla.) *Herald*

A sum of $26.75 in cash and a large quantity of fruit, vegetables, cereals, butter, towels, wash cloths, and other articles were included in the donations to the city hospital on annual gift day.

The daily collection of ashes and garbage for the past year was also donated.

Savanna (Ill.) *News*

As a pioneer and professional man Dr. Jancky was out in front. Fifty-nine years he practiced medicine, being responsible for most of the babies born in the community.

Pomeroy (Ohio) *Democrat*

Charles M. Johnson, 33, Garnas Lane, was fined $6 for an expired chauffeur's license and $6 for going the wrong way on a sticker.

Charleston (W.Va.) *Mail*

Several of the dog's ribs were broken and it was also bruised in the tussle.

Troy (Pa.) *Gazette-Register*

The baby when born should have the best of care. It should be fed on milk only from a doctor.

Los Angeles (Calif.) *Examiner*

The Lancaster City Health Department announced today that due to the increased demand for birth and death certificates they must be ordered at least one week in advance. Telephone orders are not accepted, Dr. L. L. Kersell, health commissioner, said.

Lancaster (Ohio) *Eagle-Gazette*

Countless thousands, including men, women and children, and tiny babes in arms, raced across the field.

San Francisco (Calif.) *Chronicle*

Though retired now from active mission work, he is 'doing the work of the Lord on the side' while following his earlier and more respectable trade as a boss bricklayer.

Washington (D.C.) *Star*

Mrs. Annie Mason and The Singing Troubadours wish to announce the marriage of their daughter.

Chicago (Ill.) *Tribune*

The principal effect of the storm in this city was the moving of a lot of debris from where it was to where it is.

Dunbar (W. Va.) *Advance*

He was taken to St. Luke's hospital for treatment, but left there this morning with no bones broken.

Tryon (N.C.) *Bulletin*

A baby daughter was born to Mr. and Mrs. Charles Dennis while they were in Memphis. Mr. Dennis mixed business with pleasure.

Nashville (Tenn.) *Tennessean*

Vincenzo Meile, father of the girl, was awarded, in addition, $5,000 for expenses resulting from his daughter's injury. He operates a grocery store and six other children.

Brooklyn (N.Y.) *Daily*

The children would divide their time between the living room and the kitchen where they would pop corn over the kitchen stove and bring it in to the older folks oozing with butter.

Grand Island (Nebr.) *Daily Independent*

Dogs are getting bigger, according to a leading dog manufacturer.

Duluth (Minn.) *News-Tribune*

Paul Voizs, 33, single, was electrocuted in the scrap yard of the Weirton Steel plant this morning when he picked up a live wire walking along the railroad track.

Huntington (W. Va.) *Advertiser*

Smith, Utah's 6-9 sophomore sensation, didn't see action until this part of the game, and he didn't start the second half, but he was impressive in his time out.

Albuquerque (N.M.) Journal

"Herod had such word," said Jared, "and sent forth men to slap the babes in Bethlehem."

Cincinnati (Ohio) Enquirer

Here the bridal couple stood, facing the floral setting and exchanged cows.

Modesto (Calif.) News-Herald

Steady downpours swept the western half of the state into north-central Texas.

Lubbock (Tex.) Avalanche-Journal

The dinner is to honor residents and interns who are leaving the hospital and their wives.

Buffalo (N.Y.) Evening News

As for Mrs. Kennedy's infant son, the pediatrician said he was eating well, drying well and in good general condition.

Dallas (Tex.) News

Stein was afterward sent to prison for robbing and strangling another woman without killing her.

New York (N.Y.) Herald Tribune

"A resolution to install two fire hydrants was approved by the council. The resolution followed a re-

136

port by the police department that the dog population during the past year has increased by 26."

Hackensack (N.J.) *Record*

After the literary program, refreshments were saved by the hostess.

Burlington (Vt.) *Free Press*

Mrs. Robert Whiteman, 25 West 104th Street, brought her nine-year-old daughter, Grace, before the rostrum and related how the child had been cured by prayer at the Church of Fallen Arches.

New York (N.Y.) *Times*

Just a case of being tricked by his imagination. How is he to know where the girl herself begins and her setting ends?

Pittsburgh (Pa.) *Sun Telegraph*

"It is time that I let my hair down," said the Commissioner, "and let the chips fall where they may."

Syracuse (N.Y.) *Herald-Journal*

Family difficulties lay behind John Wright's attempt to kill himself and then swim the Skunk River.

Des Moines (Iowa) *Register*

Armless though he is, Charles Vulak, fifty-five years of age, has made such a success of the begging "profession" that he has $4,053 in five different banks where he readily can lay hands on it.

Los Angeles (Calif.) *Times*

Major Peake then informed the prisoner he would be confined in the East wind.

Denver (Colo.) *Post*

A house belonging to Mr. Burdge had strayed into the road and in trying to avoid hitting it Mr. Havens struck the pole.

Asbury Park (N.J.) *Evening Press*

Kuida's skull was fractured and he was not given a chance to live by attending physicians.

Ontario (Calif.) *Daily Report*

The police did not think it necessary to put a police guard on Mrs. Franklin while she was in the maternity ward of the hospital. However, last night, she and her new baby walked out of the hospital unnoticed.

St. Louis (Mo.) *Dispatch*

Anthony Eden underwent his fourth operation to remove an obstruction in a bile duct. The canal is being opened to an ever-increasing volume of shipping.

Allentown (Pa.) *Call*

"Since silk generates static electricity," says Maj. Gen. Howard W. Doan, Deputy Surgeon General, "we have to watch the kind of underclothing our nurses wear in operating rooms."

Washington (D.C.) *Army Times*

PRESS BONERS

Miss Randall has returned from St. Louis where she went in the interest of her military business.

Owensboro (Ky.) *Messenger & Inquirer*

Many students and local fans are planning to follow the team to the scene of bottle.

Athens (Ga.) *Banner Herald*

A little baking powder added to the floor in which oysters are rolled before frying will make oysters light and fluffy.

Washington (D.C.) *News*

The audience became melted down, tears flowed freely from the eyes of the bishop and all over the audience.

Savannah (Ga.) *Morning News*

The College Y.M.C.A. was scheduled to spend Friday night at a slumber party at the new Y.W.C.A. rooms. A large number of young men will take part.

Norfolk (Nebr.) *News*

The island is a favorite spot with picneckers.

Louisville (Ky.) *Courier-Journal*

No Governor in many years has been able to love on the salary paid him, even though he is supplied with a furnished home rent free.

Petersburg (Va.) *Progress-Index*

139

His friends could give no reason why he should have committed suicide. He is single.

Stamford (Conn.) *Advocate*

Jewelry and clothing valued at from $2,000,000 to $2,500,000 belonging to Mme. Ganna Walska, wife of Harold McCormick, harvested millionaire, was held.

Lima (Ohio) *Citizen*

Lauren Bacall waited for four hours for Irving Lazar to escort her to the Billy Wilder party. Irving was taking a walk near his home when a motorcycle cop collided with his Derriere.

Houston (Tex.) *Chronicle*

He was involved in entering a home and opening suitcases and looking through the contents of women's underthings.

Hilo (Hawaii) *Tribune-Herald*

The President has been sick for several days and he is now in bed with a coed.

Salem (Ore.) *Capital Journal*

Mr. and Mrs. Fred Walker and family returned Saturday afternoon from a two weeks' tour of the west and southern part of the State. They report a fine trip with no car trouble excepting about twelve miles from Durango when Mr. Walker tore out his rear end.

Greeley (Colo.) *Tribune*

FOOTBALL SCORES:
Northwestern 20, Michigan 13
Arkansas 35, Texas 19
Alabama 42, Georgia 28
Yale 19, Vassar 0

Detroit (Mich.) *News*

Peel 1 dozen large ripe peaches, cut in slices and mash very slightly with a ford.

Oklahoma City (Okla.) *Times*

He felt the Canadian beauty at her apartment and went home.

Tampa (Fla.) *Tribune*

Arrangements have been made with members of the congregation to bring canaries to the number of fifty to the church for the six o'clock sunrise service. The birds will be placed in cakes in various parts of the church.

San Antonio (Tex.) *Express*

The Governor smoked a cigar during the interview and despite its length, appeared infatigued at its conclusion, although it had delayed his lunch nearly an hour.

St. Paul (Minn.) *Dispatch*

Knowles had been in a hospital for the last month as an habitual alcoholic. Police issued orders for hish arrest.

Philadelphia (Pa.) *Inquirer*

The truck passed over Mr. Griffin's body, but upon being taken to the hospital it was discovered that he said Thursday that in years long ago it was nothing to cut ice from two to six inches thick.

Lenoir (N.C.) *News-Leader*

The police chief promptly escorted the stranger to jail on a handhandling charge.

Lancaster (Pa.) *New Era*

The Clifton Forge Rescue Squad was called to Iron Gate for Clarence Milton, Jr., seven, who had a possible broken leg. The squad splintered his leg and removed him to the C & O Hospital.

Clifton Forge (Va.) *Review*

Alfred Watson and wife, have been living with the wife's people, have had to leave town on account of her parents having gone to live with the grandparents.

Regina (Canada) *Leader-Post*

The geologist expects to devote the first part of his stay to the study of the lower football region.

Fresno (Calif.) *Bee*

DUMPLINGS: Two cups of flour, 2 teaspoons of baking powder, ½ teaspoon of salt, one egg, beaten, ½ cup of water. Mix with a spatula and drop on boiling brother and simmer for 20 minutes without lifting the cover. If this method is followed you will have the lightest dumplings you ever ate. When I get out of the hospital I will send more recipes.

Albany (N.Y.) *Times-Union*

Tonight, after the Evening Worship Hour, the adults will meet for a "get acquainted" period. Each one is asked to bring a sandwich, the drink will be provided. This could be a very high hour together.

Atlanta (Ga.) *Church Bulletin*

He admitted the attempted rape in the presence of a Dallas News reporter.

Dallas (Tex.) *Morning News*

Representative Charles A. Eaton is an official whose words carry considerable weight. His remarks in the current issue of the American Magazine are therefore worth nothing.

Trenton (N.J.) *Evening Times*

Col. Samuel O. Wynne, Federal Prohibition Administrator, this afternoon assigned Alexander MacPhee, his deputy, and three of his most experienced agents to assist the Grand Jury bootlegging in Philadelphia.

Philadelphia (Pa.) *Bulletin*

Maloney was thrown some distance, bruising one leg severely, and opening an irrigation ditch across his scalp.

Longmont (Colo.) *Times-Call*

She was the only girl the Duke danced with. "He told me I had the most wonderful," she said later with a sigh.

Cape May (N.J.) *Star and Wave*

Heretofore there has been no charge other than a fat operating room fee of $20.

Brooksville (Fla.) *Sun*

There are already several hundred Gay Ladies in hospitals throughout Greater Boston. There is a great need for more people willing to perform this kind of work.

Boston (Mass.) *Back Bay Ledger*

Mr. and Mrs. Thomas Q. Wilson of Shadewell, Ga., are visiting their grandmother, Miss Ella Read.

Birmingham (Ala.) *Post Herald*

The Sunday school will have a party for the entire church school on the night of December 19. Make your plans not to attend.

Raleigh (N.C.) *Church Bulletin*

Gus D. Revol, well-known agent of the Cadillac Auto Company, will shortly occupy the handsome Bacher Home, 3504 Napoleon Avenue with his family, which he recently purchased.

New Orleans (La.) *Times-Picayune*

Arkansas flew in Wednesday for its date with Nebraska in the Cotton Bowl and Coach Frank Broyles said grimly, "We came to pray."

Dallas (Tex.) *News*

Mrs. Hicks states that among her favorite in recipes is making a variety of rolls. She has two small children made from the basic recipe.

Richmond-Rosenberg (Tex.) *Herald-Coaster*

Overcome by gas while taking a bath, she owes her life to the watchfulness of the janitor.

Kansas City (Mo.) *Star*

The ambulance driver reported that the victim suffered at least two broken legs.

Meade (Kan.) *Globe-Press*

The election was one of the quietest in Chicago history. Theft of one ballot-box, dynamiting of two places used as Democratic headquarters, destruction by fire of a negro church under mysterious circumstances, and the firing of a few shots were the only untoward incidents reported.

Kansas City (Mo.) *Star*

The House of Representatives complied by voting enough funds to hide 15 additional state troopers.

Boston (Mass.) *Globe*

Henry Toner was accused of insulting Mrs. Hancey on her concrete rear at her home on Tenth Street.

> Atlanta (Ga.) *Journal*

Chief McGranaghan heaped high praise on Union Leader Reporter Reg Abbott for bringing the statistics to light. "I think Reg has done a good job. His statistics show that drinking is connected with drunken driving in lots of cases."

> Manchester (N.H.) *Sunday News*

The Tuesday Night Ladies Club had a nice time at the church after their pot-luck supper. For the first time in several months all the members were pregnant.

> Atlanta (Ga.) *Church Bulletin*

Leonard told the police if the other driver had stopped a few feet behind himself, the accident could have been avoided.

> Muskogee (Okla.) *Times-Democrat*

Whether the millionaires were most interested in stocks or blondes he declined to say.

> Dallas (Tex.) *Times Herald*

Dr. Sewell said the biggest epidemic the hospital has dealt with occurred last year when influence swept Wetumpka.

> Montgomery (Ala.) *Advertiser*

Monday morning, Mrs. Hewson and her daughter, Miss Louise R. Hewson, of New York, visited Miss Gladys Tallman. The three and Miss Palmer went north to inspect the covered bridge area at West Cornwall, and to lunch and to lunch, and to lunch, and to browse around Lime Rock.

Lakeville (Conn.) *Journal*

The ancestors of the Daniel Burton family will meet on Sunday at Edgemont Park for their annual reunion.

Easton (Pa.) *Express*

There was no scrimmaging, but the men who ran with the ball were able to display much of themselves.

Cincinnati (Ohio) *Post & Times Star*

Refreshments were served and favors given the young guests who had given presents to Susan.

Bonham (Tex.) *Herald*

Ever add anchovy fillets and green olives to potato salad? God!

Las Vegas (Nev.) *Sun*

The Young Women's Overseas Auxiliary will have an all-day sewing and surgical dressing, and lunch, on Tuesday.

Pittsburgh (Pa.) *Church Bulletin*

Five Presidents with the exception of James Buchanan, who was a bachelor, were childless.

New York (N.Y.) *Sun*

It was all due to the way Mrs. Anderson stood up there on the platform and kept a tight hold on her supporters.

Minneapolis (Minn.) *Star*

James V. Bennett told Congress that Alcatraz would have to be rebuilt or replaced. A break by three darling bank robbers brought matters to a head.

Pasadena (Calif.) *Star-News-Citizen*

Many minor accidents were reported, though no serious fatalities were recorded in the immediate vicinity.

St. Louis (Mo.) *Leader*

A typisht'sh mishakesh have cancele out the execution. The law requires the warrant must be perfect.

Warren (Ohio) *Tribune Chronicle*

The marriage ceremony took place in the little town of Lignieres. It was perfumed by the Archbishop of Bourges.

St. Thomas (Canada) *Times-Journal*

Governor Ritchie was born in Richmond, Virginia, August 29, 1876, the son of Judge Albert Ritchie. He was graduated with an A.B. degree from Johns Hop-

kins University of Maryland two years later and began
to practice law in Baltimore.

Richmond (Va.) *News-Leader*

Frozen milk has been known to make children
sick. There is no dietic reason why, but it is wise to
thaw the child out very slowly and stop its use if it
has any ill effect upon the baby.

Evansville (Ind.) *Press*

President Kennedy and the First Lady are expecting their third child, it was learned from a source believed to be responsible.

Alhambra (Calif.) *Post-Advocate*

Owens was killed instantly yesterday when his
auto crashed against a utility pole after leaving Dick-
erson road, seven miles from Nashville. He was
also dead on arrival at General Hospital.

Nashville (Tenn.) *Banner*

The jury retired at 10 a.m. on May 24 and de-
liberated 24 hours before returning a verdict of guilty
of manslaughter. This conviction carries a penalty of
one to ten years in California.

Omaha (Nebr.) *World-Herald*

Residents of the flood-threatened area were advised
to remain on their toes, as the floodwaters may begin
to rise again at any moment.

Detroit (Mich.) *Free Press*

He was an engaging small dog, said an observer with a curly tail and friendly manner.

New Castle (N.Y.) *Tribune*

Cpl. Isadore Bradlyn spent the week-end with his wife, Selma. He was awarded the good-conduct medal.

Youngstown (Ohio) *Jewish Times*

Operatives of the police stolen-car department were ordered Tuesday to pick up a green roadster "driven by a good-looking blonde with wire wheels."

Tulsa (Okla.) *World*

Usually vegetables and bits of meat are left in the broth which is slightly thickened by rice, barley, or needles.

Los Angeles (Calif.) *Herald-Examiner*

Orange phosphorescent helmets were worn by the Navy players on their backs and ends.

New York (N.Y.) *Times*

Mr. Kramer was ordered to post bond pending inquest by the local crooner.

Pittsburgh (Pa.) *Press*

Montelle Watson and Marie Phillips went to country high school together in Kansas, and their marriage will stop a romance begun between them there.

Charlotte (W.Va.) *Gazette*

There is no unemployment in this district now. Every industry seems to be flourishing.

There were thirty-seven new births reported in this city last week.

Springfield (Mo.) *News*

Bill Johnston died late yesterday while riding a horse, and today word was received that his partner, James DeWitt, died at Indianapolis of the same disease.

Columbus (Ohio) *Dispatch*

Due to the recent heavy rains in Eastern North Carolina the Boy Scouts' camp, Camp Carver, is closer due to the rains knocking the dam out there.

New Bern (N.C.) *Sun-Journal*

A stray dog with the name E. G. Caldwell has been about the village for a few days.

Alma (Ark.) *Times-Herald*

Fort Bragg, located near Fayetteville, N.C., is said to be the largest distillery post in the United States.

Detroit (Mich.) *Free Press*

Since going off her diet she has been seen prominent in many places.

Nashville (Tenn.) *Tennessean*

The pregame jam at the arena was so great that extra police were called in to break up the crowd in front of the main box of ice.

Detroit (Mich.) *Times*

Whether the first-year team has the potential strength of the 1954 freshmen, Coach Bill Marx will not hazard a guess. Last year's freshman eleven won all three of its games. The Husky frosh hold a four-game advantage over the young Cougars in their past five games, the only Washington loss being the 13-7 defeat in 1953 at Pullman.

Other starters probably will include Career Boy, Gun Shot, Polly's Jet, Bold Bazooka, Lawless, Nail, Happy New Year, Call Me Lucky, Nahoda, Prince John and Espea.

Seattle (Wash.) *Times*

Miss Josie Diviny and Fred Browne were married at Hoxie, Kansas, some weeks ago. They are both highly respected and we did not suspect it until yesterday.

Wilsonville (Nebr.) *News*

A coroner's jury that celebrated three hours found that Smith shot in self-defense after Partain attacked him with a rock.

Nogales (Ariz.) *Herald*

Dr. Dublin said reports of the first 1,000 cases, submitted by Mrs. Mary Breckinridge, director of the service, showed not a single death as a direct result of childbirth. Two men had died of disorders not attributed to motherhood.

Tampa (Fla.) *Tribune*

Frieda Hempel, opera singer, entertained 15 children of seven New York patrolmen who were killed last year at a Christmas party at her home.

Plainfield (N.J.) *Courier-News*

Four highway bridges were washed out during the cloudburst. Several callers in homes in South Ryegate village were filled with water.

Montpelier (Vt.) *Argus*

Starr is accompanied by his wife. They have with them their prize-winning dog, Feng Shui, which travels on a pass on numerous bus lines and has a permit from Mexico to carry a gun in the neighboring country.

Los Angeles (Calif.) *Times*

The Navy's world commitments are such that two thirds of its men are on seat duty at all times.

Tulsa (Okla.) *World*

Mrs. La Centra was bound and gagged with adhesive tape and asked where the money was.

Boston (Mass.) *Globe*

Pour soap into earthen casserole, put bread on top, sprinkle with ¼ cup grated cheese and set in oven long enough to brown the cheese.

Rochester (N.Y.) *American*

"I've never seen anything like it," said Broyles before the game. "These people are taking this thing

153

serious." He said this as he gnawed off his fingernails up to the elbow.

Fort Smith (Ark.) *Southwest American*

Twice a bridegroom and finally a bride—at least for last night—was Miss Watson.

West Chester (Pa.) *Daily Local News*

A jury which had contained wine but which was smashed into fragments was picked up at the scene of the crash by the prosecutor and will be held as evidence.

Wheeling (W.Va.) *Intelligencer*

Forty persons here are taking treatment to prevent babies. The persons have been bitten during the past few days by dogs.

Albemarle (N.C.) *Stanly News and Press*

Persons heretofore killed or injured in the State's employment have appealed to the legislature.

Wichita (Kan.) *Daily Times*

He returned to San Diego for reassignment in the U. S. Navy. His bride will enjoy him after he is located.

Roseville (Ill.) *Press*

Several small brides were reported washed away and roads flooded.

Rochester (N.Y.) *Democrat and Chronicle*

A woman bar operator, wounded in what appeared to be an accidental shooting, was reported in what apparently was an Hospital today after stomach surgery.

New Orleans (La.) *States & Item*

The column also exhibits an ignorance to the very nature of man in relation to the scared state of marriage.

Chester (Pa.) *Delaware County Daily Times*

All members are requested to bring their wives and one other covered dish, along with table service.

Rome City (Ind.) *News*

Widow Morton has opened her sandwich shop so don't forget to stop in when you are in want of a good sandwich or something.

Van Buren (Ark.) *Press Argus*

Phil Assmus, who formerly was there, is playing at his old position of right tickle, behind Dick Pomygalski.

New York (N.Y.) *Times*

The former airport, operated by the Association, is one of the most dangerous from the standpoint of wires as a large series of steel towers carry unusually powerful wives past the east side of the field.

Indianapolis (Ind.) *Star*

Col. Charles A. Lindbergh and Henry Breckenridge, his counsel, who took off in an airplane from Curtiss Field, New York, this afternoon, were forced to land on a farmer near here late today because of a dense fog.

Chicago (Ill.) *Tribune*

Madalynne has a natural taste for classic city clothes. She's on the tail side—a well filled out size 16.

New York (N.Y.) *Herald Tribune*

Zelda Perkins came home June 4th after completing a year's work at the University of Tennessee, Knoxville. She is taking a home economics course along with some education.

Crossville (Tenn.) *Chronicle*

She is a singer of unusual attributes . . . she will please any audience by the charm of her personality and the excellence of her aft.

Redlands (Calif.) *Facts*

Owing to the lack of space and the rush of editing this issue, several births and deaths will be postponed until next week.

Burlington (Iowa) *Hawk-Eye*

Moved by Commissioner Doherty that the report of E. T. Burke, Fire Chief, be approved and placed on fire.

Ottawa (Ill.) *Republican-Times*

PRESS BONERS

Sportsmen of this county are sharing with others in this state and with conservation leaders in many parts of the country the privilege of helping to save the noted Anderson Hill Wild Wife refuge.

Hutchinson (Minn.) *Leader*

Did you know that you can take a coat hanger and a pair of pliers or wire snippers and cut a piece of wire (from the bottom of the hanger, about 12 inches long, and bend it into the shape of a "U"). This means it will look like an old horseshoe.

Lancaster (Pa.) *New Era*

Mrs. W. K. Price greeted the guests at the door, and the receiving line was formed by J. Sam Hinson, Mrs. J. J. Shuman, R. M. Cline, Mrs. W. G. Helms, Mr. and related, the 10 laundries in Charlette as participants in the special enterprise agree to wash and iron Mrs. Spencer, their younger son, John, and daughter, Anna.

Charlotte (N.C.) *Observer*

A check at the local swimming pool revealed some startling figures.

Portland (Ind.) *Graphic*

The C-47, carrying a planeload of chorus girls bound for a USO destination to entertain troops, was forced down in a jungle somewhere in Africa . . . However, all parsons aboard were reported safe.

St. Louis (Mo.) *Post-Dispatch*

For the second year in a row, she made the list as one of the ten best-breasted women in the United States.

Chicago (Ill.) *Tribune*

He gave his eldest son a liberal education. The rest he brought up respectably.

Norwich (Conn.) *Bulletin*

"My son-in-law hit his head working in a factory," she said. "Now he writes stories. He has a typewriter."

Denver (Colo.) *Post*

As he flung the blazing oil-stove out of the window, Mr. Perkins stumbled over a chair and sat down amidst some ignited shavings on the floor, the flame from which caught his clothes. By quick action and a ready wit he escaped with his life, but his trousers were burned almost beyond recognition.

Woodbury (N.J.) *Times*

Mrs. Shirley Baxter, who went deer hunting with her husband, is very proud that she was able to shoot a fine buck as well as her husband.

Clinton County (Mich.) *Republican-News*

Wash the garment with tepid water, using neuter soaps for wool. Do not rub nor twist it, rinse it abundantly with cold water, dry it in the shadow. Still, in order to have the piece unshrinked, the brightness of colours, the softness of stitch, it is advisable to dry-clean.

Albany (N.Y.) *Times-Union*

Nothing gives a greater variety to the appearance of a house than a few undraped widows.

(New York, N.Y.) *House & Garden*

The Duchess of Windsor, looking not a bit worn from her recent bout with pneumonia, dining with the Duke and best friend Charlie Cushing and striking Sloan Simpson at Le Pavillon.

New York (N.Y.) *Journal-American*

Two or more persons using same private pool, charge for second and each additional person, with or without bathing suit, .50.

Hinchley (Ill.) *Review*

Captain Belanger, who set out to fly to Paris in an aeroplane yesterday was compelled to return to Pau because of the defective lubrication of his companions who started with him.

Montreal (Canada) *Gazette*

Then there's the department store that advertised a maternity dress that will make the mother-to-be look 'strikingly feminine.'

San Francisco (Calif.) *Examiner*

In deciding in favor of the new senior girls, Professor Robert declared he has spent some time considering the issue from every possible ankle.

Phoenix (Ariz.) *American*

The 24-year-old singer broke off an engagement to sin in Paris for the thrill of performing at the White House.

Three Rivers (Mich.) *Commercial*

The Times is late this week. The trouble started in a cornfield, maybe years ago. From there it reached our linotype. Yet the trouble lies not with the machine. You see, the corn grew, fermented, aged in the wood and finally reached our operator.

Prestonburg (Ky.) *Floyd County Times*

He and his wife were lowered to safety by Rescue Unit I of the fire department. The dame was said to be considerable.

Louisville (Ky.) *Courier-Journal*

John Yorke, who recently shot and killed Bert Evans while hunting deer out of season, pleaded guilty to a charge of illegal hunting and was fined $25 by United States Commissioner C. Clausen.

Petersburg (Alaska) *Herald*

Sweeping over Pennsylvania, Hurricane Gracie dumped up to three inches of rain in some isolated pots.

Eau Claire (Wisc.) *Telegram*

After the sun goes down here there are practically no recreational facilities for those who are not married.

Sacramento (Calif.) *Bee*

The next thing the novice must accomplish is to learn to breathe easily and naturally under water.

Mobile (Ala.) *News-Item*

The winner of Saturday night's competition was unheralded veterinary student from Ohio State, Jerry Welborn. And he missed by a whiskey becoming the fourth man in history to vault 15 feet.

Rochester (N.Y.) *Times-Union*

Adlai Stevenson cut short his visit in London and took the first planet home.

Nashville (Tenn.) *Banner*

Corsages of gardenias marked the places of Mrs. Champlin and Mrs. Cherry, and nosegays of panties were at the places of the other guests.

Raleigh (N.C.) *Times*

One of the most upsetting factors in many a hopeful teacher's attempt at ability grouping is the fact that after the job is carefully done we find a number of really poor students in the faster groups and a number of really excellent students in the really poor students in the faster groups and a number of really poor students in the faster groups and a number of really excellent students in the slower groups.

(Madison, Wisc.) *Journal of Education*

Leonard Bernstein and the New York Philharmonic Orchestra won the hearts of 6000 British children today in spite of the echoes that resounded through Royal Albert Hall Hall Hall Hall.

New York (N.Y.) *Times*

Meddling with the instruments of the musicians was a most inappropriate thing to do.

Van Buren (Ark.) *Press Argus*

And in Heaven, we may find people not just from our own earth but from millions of other planets like our own. Oh, it is possible that such people might differ from us in height. For we find here on this planet that savages are usually smaller than us more educated races.

Ogden (Utah) *Standard-Examiner*

"I personally enjoy your paper as much as my husband."

Geary (Okla.) *Star*

A burning shingle from the barn fell on Mrs. Anna Noonan's neck and inflicted a severe burn. The loss is only partly covered by insurance.

Worcester (N.Y.) *Times*

A sportsman before being allowed to kill an elk, must be a bull with horns.

Salt Lake City (Utah) *Salt Lake Telegram*

The heavy rain, this week, has swollen all the small streams and Marion Lieff.

Middletown (N.Y.) *Times Herald-Record*

162

First as a newspaper columnist and now as one of the lovelies in a smart New York night club, Marguerite McDonnell has learned that good lines pay off. She was doing all right writing for a paper in Chicago, her home town, and later in St. Petersburg, Fla., when she decided she was just the type for show business. She hopes to make enough money to afford to return to journalism.

Buffalo (N.Y.) *Courier-Express*

The Colgate-Palmolive Company, at a press luncheon in New York April 30, announced that it will contribute 10 cents to the Olympic Fund for the first 1,000,000 box tops or wrappers collected from specified soaps, detergents and toiletries between now and July 15.

New York (N.Y.) *Times*

About one third of all passengers flying between London and Paris travel by air.

Cleveland (Ohio) *Plain Dealer*

Mrs. Ralph K. Davies chatted with Mrs. Louis Benoist, who wore a large aqua-colored hat to ward off the sun and Mrs. Clarence Musto.

Redwood City (Calif.) *Tribune*

Ten percent of everything American women put into Maiderform bras each year goes for advertising.

Bayonne (N.J.) *Times*

Not only has the Plymouth boy made good amongst his fraternity friends, but he was listed among nine of

163

the university's athletes to receive the coveted letter of the ien Ubetaoin shrd cmf vhg vbgkvv.

Plymouth (Mass.) *Old Colony Memorial*

In the back of the orchestra Walter Sneed played up a storm.

Birmingham (Ala.) *Post Herald*

The Jefferson Square Improvement club offers a prize of five dollars for the best poem on the Northern Pacific crossing at South 17th and Pacific.

Profanity barred.

Tacoma (Wash.) *News Tribune*

It is nearly as hard to correct a typographical error as to get a woman unpregnant.

Van Buren (Ark.) *Press Argus*

KNOW YOUR FIRE DEPARTMENT
In case of fire call ID 3-5211
7:30 P. M.
Hamburg (Ark.) *Ashley County Leader*

The entire organization has not been completed, but they were inviting all of the Forest Hills club members who wanted to try their hand at shooting clay pigeons and the general public.

Long Island (N.Y.) *Newsday*

In several cases, north and east of the bay area, roads were being operated as one-way highways, and motorists were required to wear tire chains.

Oakland (Calif.) *Tribune*

Mrs. Donaldson, who with her daughter welcomed her guests, was surprised at the unusual number of acceptances, in proportion to the number of invitations sent out, and she attributed the swilling crowds to her daughter's recent artistic and literary fame.

Boston (Mass.) *Transcript*

What is the "Catnip Club"? Yes, that is the paramount topic in the smart circles of local society today, many having received swank invitations to the opening party Friday evening in the beautiful bathroom of the Thomas Jefferson Hotel.

Birmingham (Ala.) *News-Age Herald*

Dear Mester Hines: I got your letter about what I owe you. Now be pachent. I aint forgot you. Pleez wait. Whun some fools pay me I pay you. If this was judgment day and you wus no more prepared to meet your Master as I am to meet your account, you sure would have to go to hell. Trusting you will do this. I am yours truly.

Benkelman (Nebr.) *Post*

Mrs. Williams was acclaimed champion rolling pin thrower; her husband won the 100-yard dash and the chicken race.

Pasadena (Calif.) *Independent*

Among the first passengers were Mrs. Mabel Willebrandt, who is now associated with an aviation corporation as Washington counsel. Mrs. Willebrandt carried a quart bottle of water taken from the Atlantic ocean, which she poured into the Pacific upon arrival in Kansas City.

Quincy (Ill.) *Herald-Whig*

To prevent those odd suntans caused by the cut of some high fashion bathing suits, alternate with a suit that exposes any area covered up by the other.

Detroit (Mich.) *Free Press*

Brewer Hall, which will house 144 men, was completed in September of 1958. The structure of Brewer Hall is almost identical to that of Blanton Hall in that it contains units of two bedrooms with connecting bath and closet space for four girls.

Kirksville (Mo.)
Northeast Missouri State Teachers College

As an encore, Miss Brown played the old favorite, "Carry Me Back to Old Virginity."

Winfield (Kan.) *Courier*

Miss Simpson is well known as a great hobbyist. For years she has been developing several of her hubbys to the point where they are now self supporting.

Cleveland (Ohio) *Press & News*

He has turned down an offer to coach a six-man AAU touring track team on a trip to Trinidad. Cuties at Nebraska keep him too busy to accept, he said.

Beatrice (Nebr.) *Sun*

If, in spite of precautions, you should one day detect the acrid, penetrating odor of a chimney fire, pour five or ten pounds of table salt down the chimney and at the same time turn in an alarm of fire.

Lovington (N.M.) *Leader*

Mrs. Gordon Harris, Mrs. Hugh Gregory, Bill Knight and Harold Singleton went to Pickens Tuesday ramp hunting. They all came back loaded.

Braxton (W.Va.) *Democrat*

Take your work seriously. First be acurrate, then be quick.

Chicago (Ill.) *Tribune*

When a clerk wants to look up zebra on a rotary card file, she doesn't go hunting for the "Z" cards, instead she presses a button, the file revolves and "X" section stops directly in front of her.

St. Louis (Mo.) *Globe-Democrat*

Notice to the public: Due to the reorganization of our mail order department, and to our employees unfamiliarity with the new speed-up procedures for mail orders, we find it necessary to advise that mail orders will not be shipped as promptly as in the past.

New York (N.Y.) *Times*

The best way to get along as a modern secretary is to pick up your notebook and pencil, and answer the buzzard promptly.

Kansas City (Mo.) *Star*

Bishop Beecher loves to quote the following entry in Bishop Grave's diary: "Went duck-hunting with Beecher this morning; killed 12; baptized three in the evening."

Omaha (Nebr.) *World-Herald*

Three children died in a cloudburst near Memphis, Texas, as floods swept that section of the Southwest. Beneficial rains also fell in the San Angelo area.

San Angelo (Tex.) *Standard-Times*

The bust is narrow, flat and rectangular, and is rarely seen before evening.

Charlotte (N.C.) *Observer*

Mrs. Fletcher and her husband designed their headpieces from paper bags. Mrs. Fletcher was the horse's head and her husband followed her behind the entire evening.

Fort Smith (Ark.) *News*

Generally, in business the girl with the low-cut dress is looked down on.

Detroit (Mich.) *Times*

More than 5000 high school girls, most of whom are interested primarily in the homes they expect to ruin in the future, will gather here next week-end.

Oklahoma City (Okla.) *Times*

Beethoven was a great musician. He had ten children, and practiced on a spinster in the attic.

Philadelphia (Pa.) *Bulletin*

We pitched our camp on a high bank among some trees and while my companion retired to his hammock and kept guard I went off to investigate the lady of the land.

Los Angeles (Calif.) *Times*

Mrs. Jessup was so clearly the master in the first five games of the singles match that the event began to take on the attributes of a complete rout. Miss Palfrey was obviously nervous and her shoes were not coming off successfully.

New York (N.Y.) *Herald Tribune*

His hobbies include hunting, skiing, tinkering with his blue Chrysler and Nancy.

Laurel (Mont.) *Outlook*

Fred Call, a national forest fire guard, recently saved a giant tree by crawling into the hollow part, which was aflame, and cutting away the burning wood. First he chopped the tree down.

Great Falls (Mont.) *Leader*

The lightning flash first hit the air conditioner, jumped to the TV and then hit Miss Simmons in the rear as she was leaning over to pick up a book. It injured her somewhat.

Muskogee (Okla.) *Times-Democrat*

Two nice young misses, nearly dressed, and with tennis rackets walking as near the middle of the road as possible and laughing at all the motorists forced to stop for them.

Birch Bay (Wash.) *News*

An Arkansas minister said today that there are more than 3,000,000 nudists in the United States and he would like to cover up every one of them. "Just think of it," said the Rev. ——— of Fort Smith, "a nudist for every Boy Scout in America."

New York (N.Y.) *Daily News*

Mr. Darrell Spencer, school board member, stated that starting with the spring semister that parents ain't going to be allowed to visit pupils during school hours.

South Bend (Ind.) *News-Times*

A person can undergo silent confinement for two daysandtwonightsinavery small space without effect on his ability to learn.

New York (N.Y.) *Times*

The Game Commission of Pennsylvania has made a thorough review of the mammas of Pennsylvania and finds that there are more than fifty species.

Clarion (Pa.) *Democrat*

Joe Newton, Auburn's All-SEC basketball center, has his big day Saturday. The home folks at Fayette have proclaimed it "Joe Nelson Day."

Birmingham (Ala.) *Post-Herald*

West Walworth Volunteer Fire Department will blow the siren 15 minutes before the start of each fire.

Ontario (N.Y.) *Wayne County Mail*

Next summer, according to a French astrologer, the world will suffer from intense heat, followed by a terrific explosion, and will come to an end. In that case it might be wise to start now, and get as far away from Houston as possible.

Detroit (Mich.) *News*

Last evening the Tennis Club ball was held at the Community Hall. Seldom has there been so splendid a display of beaux and bellies.

Bridgewater (Canada) *Bulletin*

The number of cavities in Philadelphia school children has been cut in half.

Buffalo (N.Y.) *Courier-Express*

Merapi, the great volcano which has been dormant for eighty years, burst into violent eruption and arrived today to pass the holidays with his parents, the Rev. R. H. Coffman and Mrs. Coffman.

Saratoga (N.Y.) *Saratogian*

For the second year, Miss Martin won Honorable Mention for her colorful marigolds and lush poses.

Lincoln (Nebr.) *Star*

The husband explained to the doorman that when they came out he found that they had left their daughter's handbag and wife's behind.

Mansfield (Ohio) *Tribune*

The French press stormed when they learned that she had become the owner of the "Chateau de Taurine", and the title of Countless, which went along with the old pile.

New York (N.Y.) *Evening Journal*

At St. Louis, over a loud-speaker system, she told the throng with a smile: "I am only here for a little while. I can only say a brief word. I am very pleased to have a chance to say hell, good-by and good luck."

Houston (Tex.) *Post*

Cuba's fiery red national bank president, Ernesto 'Che' Guevara, flew from Moscow to East Berlin to meet more Soviet bloc Heads.

Cleveland (Ohio) *Press*

If your skin is not liable to be sensitive, rub the arms gently with pumice stone. This will take them right off.

Chicago (Ill.) *Tribune*

Miss Germany is noted for the platinum blonde hair which hangs to her lips.

Erie (Pa.) *Daily Times*

In the absence of Mrs. Debbley, Mr. George Fontaine undressed the D.A.R. Tuesday afternoon. Mr. Fontaine showed his familiarity with the subjects under discussion by going thoroughly over the outlines of the D.A.R. for the year.

Greenfield (Miss.) *News*

Throwing both arms around her, he kissed her upon her reappearance.

Pittsburgh (Pa.) *Press*

Hearing a noise on his front porch, Joseph Gigliotti picked it up and threw it towards the street.

Grafton (W.Va.) *Sentinel*

A girl who is seventeen is much more of a woman than is a boy who is seventeen.

New York (N.Y.) *Journal-American*

Germans have invented a folding canoe, seating two persons that can be rolled into a bundle four feet long by six inches in diameter.

Goldfield (Nev.) *News*

Hagan ran his finger through his hair and took out a cigar.

Indianapolis (Ind.) *Star*

The Duchess handled the launching beautifully, smashing the champagne bottle against the prow with the aplomb of an expert. The crowd cheered as she majestically slid down the greasy runway into the sea.

New York (N.Y.) *Times*

The father searched himself by boat for his daughter.

New York (N.Y.) *Journal-American*

He described the fitting of the Snark, on the day before the flight, with a "destructor", a rectangular rod about four feet long, attached to the root of the missile's wing. He said that if something were to go attachet m-sreotofalih dteot7ox zhsile's wing. He said that if something were o go wrong during he atachedt of the root o ft he millisl's wing. He said that if something were to go wrong . . .

Utica (N.Y.) *Press*

The panties at City Hall Park are at their prettiest now.

Jackson (Mo.) *Pioneer*

Again Peyton Place

by ROGER FULLER

A vital, moving
story of the
younger
generation
in Peyton Place,
the town made
famous by the
best-selling novels of
GRACE METALIOUS

75196/75¢

Other titles by Grace Metalious:

NO ADAM IN EDEN . . . . .75002/75¢
PEYTON PLACE . . . . .75087/75¢

If your bookseller does not have these titles, you may
order them by sending retail price, plus 10¢ for mailing and handling to: MAIL SERVICE DEPARTMENT,
POCKET BOOKS, A Division of Simon & Schuster,
Inc., 1 West 39th St., New York, N.Y. 10018. Not
responsible for orders containing cash. Please send
check or money order.

PUBLISHED BY
POCKET BOOKS

PEARL S. BUCK

BUCK

Death in the Castle

A Novel
of Suspense

"Chilling,
Thrilling"
—Boston Herald

50288/50¢

Other titles by Pearl S. Buck:

DRAGON SEED . . . . .75123/75¢·

THE GOOD EARTH . . . . .50023/50¢

THE LIVING REED . . . . .75023/75¢

THE MOTHER . . . . .50153/50¢

MY SEVERAL WORLDS . . . . .75038/75¢

PAVILION OF WOMEN . . . . .50026/50¢

If your bookseller does not have these titles, you may
order them by sending retail price, plus 10¢ for mailing and handling to: MAIL SERVICE DEPARTMENT,
POCKET BOOKS, A Division of Simon & Schuster,
Inc., 1 West 39th St., New York, N.Y. 10018. Not
responsible for orders containing cash. Please send
check or money order.

PUBLISHED BY
POCKET BOOKS